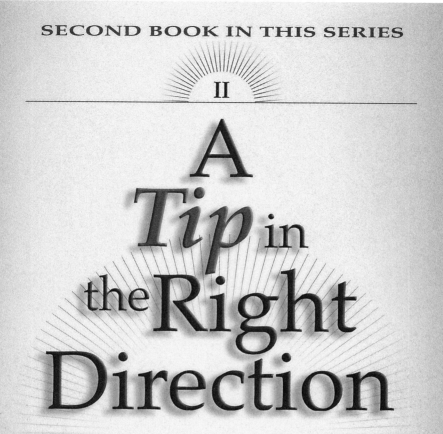

II

A *Tip* in the Right Direction

Positive Insights to Help You Learn and Grow

Robert A. Rohm, Ph.D.

Foreword by Dan T. Cathy

President, Chick-fil-A® Corporation

Robert A. Rohm Ph.D.

II
SECOND BOOK IN THIS SERIES

A
Tip in
the Right
Direction

Robert A. Rohm, Ph.D.

Personality
INSIGHTS
PRESS

Editor – Beth McLendon
Layout and Graphics – Pedro Gonzales
Title: Deborah Mullen

Published by Personality Insights, Inc.

P.O. Box 28592 • Atlanta, GA 30358-0592

First Edition, October 2004
Second Edition, August 2005
Third Edition, February 2013

1.800.509.DISC • www.personalityinsights.com

ISBN: 0-9741760-3-6

Printed in the United States of America

Table of Contents:

This book is dedicated to my mother, Katherine Rohm. She has been my biggest fan throughout my life! That kind of support will do wonders in a person's life.

I often hear people talking about their poor self-image. Let me share with you the power a mother can have in this area throughout the life of her child. Because of my mother, I probably suffer from having a self-image that is too good!

When I was growing up, my mother reminded me daily that God loved me, and that he had a wonderful plan for my life. She told me that I was smart and tall and nice-looking and a leader. Those compliments made me feel special. Whether for good or bad, it made me feel like I could do just about anything I set my mind on doing. Those qualities that she instilled in me during my formative years have remained with me throughout my lifetime.

It is funny. . . I honestly do not feel in my heart that I am better than anyone else. But, I do feel special. I do not think I am smarter or taller or better looking or a better leader than another person. But, I do feel that I received greater confidence and direction as a result of my mother's compliments in these areas. In addition, I do not believe God loves me more than he does you or any other person for that matter. But, I do believe that he loves me very much.

See what I mean? All of those blessings are in my life as a direct result of having a mother that believed in me. That is why I wanted to dedicate this book to my mother, Katherine Rohm.

Foreword

Over the years, I have known Dr. Robert Rohm in a variety of situations. But, perhaps the place I have enjoyed seeing him the most is at his favorite restaurant in Hapeville, Georgia: The Chick-fil-A® Dwarf House restaurant!

Long before he became "Dr. Rohm," Robert began coming in as a regular customer at our family restaurant way back in 1967, where the product Chick-fil-A® was birthed. He has often said that the Dwarf House was his last stop before he went next door to the airport to leave on a trip. Also, the Dwarf House was his first stop when he returned to Atlanta. We like those kind of satisfied customers in our Chick-fil-A® family! He became a self-appointed member of the Chick-fil-A® Raving Fan Club, often referring to his dining experiences in talks across the country.

This is the second "Tip" book in the *Tip in the Right Direction* series. Dr. Rohm offers practical, helpful suggestions in order to add wisdom to a person's life. I believe you will find these tips to be inspiring, informational and uplifting. This book will help you to make wise choices and live the life God designed for you!

Eat more chicken!

Dan T. Cathy,
President and Chief Operating Officer
Chick-fil-A®, Inc.
Atlanta, Georgia

Acknowledgments

No project, especially a book, is ever the result of one person's efforts. It just requires too much time and energy. Therefore, I want to always acknowledge those who faithfully help me bring forth new books for the public.

First, I want to thank my editor, Beth McLendon, for doing such an excellent job in proofreading and arranging all of these chapters. As you may know, I write a "Tip of the Week" every week. Usually the tip is centered on some burning issue or topic that is currently happening in my own life. That makes for good, interesting writing, but it can create a somewhat "disjointed" book unless someone arranges the topics in some kind of coherent order. That someone is Beth. Thank you, Beth, for doing such a great job!

I want to thank Pedro Gonzalez, our graphic designer here at Personality Insights, Inc. He constantly keeps coming up with new, fresh ideas that make our products look spectacular. His ideas and creativity never cease to amaze me. Whoever said, "You can't judge a book by looking at its cover," evidently had not met Pedro! My gifts are in the spoken word, while Pedro's gifts are more artistic in nature. Put that together, and you end up with a book that is pleasing to the eye and heart!

Finally, I want to thank, you, the reader, for all that you have contributed to my life. If it were not for you, I would have no one to stand up and talk to! I don't know if you have ever thought about it before, but no teacher ever achieved greatness without being challenged by various students. The student's role is the one that prepares the teacher to either learn to excel or live life in boredom. Your comments, smiles, words of encouragement and helpful suggestions have given me the drive and energy to keep helpful information coming your way. And for that I want to say, "Thank you!" I am indeed blessed and grateful to you, the reader.

God bless each and every one of you!

A helpful "Tip"
before reading this book:

Many of the tips found in this book relate to the **DISC** Model of Human Behavior. In order for you to be up-to-date and current in your understanding of the information in this book, we thought it would be helpful to provide you with a brief overview of the Model of Human Behavior before you begin.

GET THE PICTURE

Most people have predictable patterns of behavior and specific personality types. There are four basic personality types, also known as temperaments. The four types are like four parts of a pie. Before looking at each of the four parts, let's look at the pie in two parts. These two parts are designated as **outgoing** and **reserved**. Think of it this way: some people are more outgoing, while others are more reserved.

Outgoing people are more active and optimistic. *Reserved* types are more passive and careful. One type is not better than the other. Both types of behavior are needed, and both are important. Outgoing types need to learn how to be more steady and cautious. Reserved types need to learn how to be more dominant and inspiring.

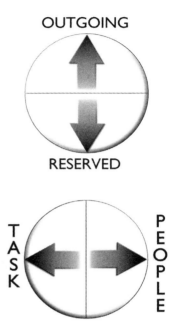

There is another way to divide the pie. It can be divided into *task-oriented* and *people-oriented*. Some people are more task-oriented, and some are more relationship-oriented.

Task-oriented types need to learn to relate better to others and become more interactive and sharing. *People-oriented* individuals need to learn to be more focused on doing tasks or things. They need to be more directing and correcting.

Now, we can have a pie divided into four parts. We can visualize the four parts: *D*, *I*, *S* and *C*. Those people who we say are predominately *"D"* types are outgoing and task-oriented. Those who we say are predominately *"I"* types are

outgoing and people-oriented. Those who we say are predominately "*S*" types are reserved and people-oriented. Those who we say are predominately "*C*" types are reserved and task-oriented.

The "*D*" type can be described with words like: Dominant, Direct, Demanding, Decisive, Determined and Doer.

The "*I*" type can be described with words like: Inspiring, Influencing, Inducing, Interactive, Impressive and Interested in people.

The "*S*" type can be described with words like: Supportive, Steady, Stable, Sweet, Sensitive and Status Quo.

The "*C*" type can be described with words like: Cautious, Calculating, Competent, Consistent, Contemplative and Careful.

D = Dominant
I = Inspiring
S = Supportive
C = Cautious

No one is purely a "*D*" or an "*I*" or an "*S*" or a "*C*". Everyone is a unique blend of these four types. If someone says that he is an "*I* / *D*" personality blend, that means that he is highest in the traits of the "*I*" (Inspiring type), and that he is next highest in the traits of the "*D*" (Dominant type). This, of course, is true of the other traits, as well.

Robert A. Rohm Ph.D.

Introduction

I once heard that motivation is a lot like bathing, because it is something you need to do every day. I wholeheartedly agree with that concept! Yesterday's bath will do little for you today...and what motivated you in the past probably needs a fresh approach to your life today. That is the main concept behind this book.

Each week, I focus on growing in one area or aspect of my own personal life. I write a "Tip of the Week" that defines or further explains that concept. The purpose of the "Tip" is to give greater clarity to the highlighted area of personal growth. By using stories, examples and illustrations, I have found a way to help people gain more insight into how to "do life" more appropriately and more successfully.

My first "Tip" book was well received. Therefore, I thought it would be a good idea to continue the series. This is the second set of 52 tips, one for each week, to help give readers guidance and food for thought along life's path.

Most people are extremely busy and have little time to read long books. This becomes especially true when readers are simply trying to get some quick motivation...or a quick shower. Therefore, these tips have been written in "bite-size" quantities for busy people. Since the purpose of this book is to help provide quick motivation for readers, most chapters are only two or three pages in length. These tips are short enough that people can easily reread each tip several times during the week in order to fully gain the truths contained within it.

As I mentioned in the first "Tip" book, these tips are not about rocket science. They are about common sense, good sense, "horse sense," being street smart and being wise. That same approach continues in this second volume as well.

So, enjoy your on-going journey through life. Stay motivated on a daily basis!

Thank you and God bless you!

Robert A. Rohm Ph.D.

Every day is an opportunity to start fresh again.

Have you ever stopped to realize how wonderful it is to get to start over? Do you remember when you were a child, and you made a mistake while playing marbles or some other game? If you called out "slippits" or "do-over" you were able to start your turn all over again. Even today, I know a lot of people who still use the "mulligan" rule when playing golf. If you hit the ball into the woods or into a creek, etc., you get to use your one "mulligan" and act as if that error never occurred. New beginnings are a wonderful part of life.

Every day is a new day. Every week is a new week. Every month is a new month, and every year is a new year. God designed it that way. He must like the concept of getting a fresh start. There are also new beginnings within new beginnings. For example, we even have four seasons in each year to give us the feeling that there is a new beginning taking place during different times of the year. Spiritually speaking, God even thought up the concept of starting your whole life over. It is called being "born again!"

I like the fact that we get to start over. Many times the only thing we can carry into our new opportunity to start over is our experiences of the things we have learned in the past. That is a good thing! When we start over with the wisdom we have gained from our experiences in the past, we can walk into our future more confidently.

I think I understand the reason why every day has 24 hours in it. There are three eight - hour segments in each day: eight hours to work, eight hours to take care of your-self mentally, physically, spiritually and socially, and then eight hours to take a long nap to get over everything that happened to you in the first two eight - hour segments!

Have you ever noticed that when you wake up every morning, regardless of how difficult things were the day before, it seems as though you have a fresh willingness to start all over again? My father often said, "Let's sleep on this issue. Things will look different tomorrow." When I was young, I didn't understand what he meant, but I have grown and matured to the place that it makes perfect sense to me now. After a good night's sleep, everything does look a little different.

Each day the sun sets on all of our problems as well as all of the mistakes that we made for that day. After we have rested mentally, physically and emotionally, we are renewed and ready to face the next day. Again, this is all a part of the Creator's plan. Even if you wake up with the same challenges that you had the previous day, you now have a fresh outlook on life, because you get a brand-new start. You begin to think, "I can do it. I can keep going. I can face another day!" It is a wonderful thing to realize that we are cooperating with everything in creation when we renew our strength and begin again fresh each day.

Tip: Every day is an opportunity
to start fresh again.

2

Make it a practice of calling ahead!

We live in a truly remarkable world. Modern technology has made life so much easier and better for all of us! Air conditioning, central heat, running water, clean bathrooms, fax machines, electricity, airplanes, telephones, etc. are all things that make life easier and more convenient for us. I have often thought how grateful I am that I was not one of the pilgrims. I would have died during that first bitterly cold winter! To me, "roughing it" is the hot tub at the Marriott!

I think the item that helps make my life the most productive is the telephone. It helps me stay in touch with my family, friends and business associates. But more than anything else, it helps me to be able to call ahead, so I can use my time wisely.

Recently, I was in Kansas City. The night before I was to depart, I discovered I would need to change my flight plans. I called the airlines to see how the flights looked for the next day. They told me everything was wide open. I was originally scheduled to fly out at 8:30 a.m. the next morning back to Atlanta. They told me that if I missed my 8:30 a.m. flight, I could come on to the airport, and I could catch a later flight. After my meeting the next morning, I called the airlines. They told me the 11:55 a.m. flight was wide open, and that I could reschedule to that flight for a small fee over the phone, or I could just do it at the airport when I got there. I decided to do it over the phone ahead of time just to be safe. Sure enough, when I got to the airport, there was mass confusion. One flight had been cancelled due to engine trouble, so everyone was being loaded on the 11:55 a.m. flight, and now it was oversold! However, since I had called and worked out all those last minute details... ahead of time, I was confirmed and ready to go!

When I was growing up, the telephone company had ads on television and radio to encourage people to use the yellow pages. There was a little catchy tune that they sang to us, "Let your fingers do the walking through the yellow pages. Find it quick; find it fast; find it now!"

The whole idea behind that ad campaign was to promote the idea of using the yellow pages to call ahead to make your life easier and better. (I realize that it was also an incentive to encourage business owners to buy an ad in the yellow pages!) The concept behind the ad was correct. Rather than working harder, why not begin to learn to work smarter?

Over the years, I have discovered something very

interesting. People are human! They mean well, but they sometimes forget or change their plans. Before I go anywhere that is important to me, I have learned to call ahead and see if the store is open or to check on their business hours or to confirm that the person I am meeting is actually there. How many times have you ever gotten to a restaurant only to think to yourself, "Why didn't I call ahead and make a reservation?" In other words, I have learned that calling ahead is a valuable habit to develop.

This week, I want to challenge you to put this tip into action. Call ahead before you go out to an appointment or to do something. Watch how you feel when you realize you just saved yourself from experiencing a big challenge or headache!

Tip: Make it a practice of calling ahead!

3

The D-I-S-C information is some of the most versatile information that you will ever process.

Many of you have heard me say that the D-I-S-C information is the third most valuable information that I possess as a human being. I continue to believe that! (The first most valuable is my spiritual relationship to God, and the second is my Biblical information and knowledge. But, after that, DISC is it!) Allow me to explain further.

Over the years, I have taught a lot of different information. I was a schoolteacher, director of curriculum, a department head, a supervisor and an administrator. I have taught, or been associated with, every academic discipline that you can imagine. But, to this day, I have never seen anything like the intense interest I observe in people when they began to really grasp the DISC information.

Recently, we had another advanced DISC training program in Atlanta. As the group introduced themselves, they each shared some of the applications of how they have been implementing the DISC concepts. This group represented a wide variety of vocations and many different personal interests. They listed teambuilding, education - helping children understand themselves and others, communication skills, staff training, organizational growth, leadership models, ministry - understanding spiritual gifts, D.N.A. (Discovering Natural Abilities) , marriage seminars, child rearing, time management skills, human resource skills, personal counseling and increasing sales through better customer satisfaction. All those ideas were out of one class of attendees. And, I can think of even more applications of the DISC material than those listed!

As I said before, I have never seen anything like the power of this information and how it can make a difference in nearly every area of your life if you simply apply it (with practice) on a daily basis. Remember this key concept: the one who knows the information is responsible for applying it – not the one who does not know it! In others words, the ball is in your court!

Recently, I was talking to my high *"D"* daughter, Rachael. She made the comment to me that life would not make as much sense without this information. When I asked her why she thought that, she said to me, "Because the truth is that all day every day, you come in contact with people, and without this information your reality (or perception of people) will be extremely frustrating!" I totally agree.

Regardless of what you do each day, let me once again encourage you to apply the DISC information to your daily life. There is not a lot of knowledge that is as broad based as DISC, so remember to use it to the fullest extent.

DISC works. It is powerful. It will make a difference in all that you do!

Tip: The D-I-S-C information is some of the most versatile information that you will ever process.

4

Be character driven, not personality driven.

I love personality information. It has affected my life for the better so very much… and in turn has affected the lives of other people as well. Over a million people have come directly in contact with Personality Insights and the D-I-S-C information. For that and much more, I am extremely grateful.

Our personality drives us to go through life the way we do. The *"D"* types love to be in charge and make things happen. The *"I"* types are the life of the party. They love to talk with everyone they meet. The *"S"* types are gentle, kind and sweet. They prefer peace and harmony over conflict every time. The *"C"* types are smart. They love details and accuracy. The world is a better place, because they keep improving things. All four types of personality styles are important, and all four types are needed. However, there is something far more important than personality styles.

What I want to remind you of this week is the fact

that your personal character is far more valuable than your personality style. Although your personality style "colors" everything you do, there is something you must add to your personality style in order to give it true success. That one additional ingredient is personal character.

When Saddam Hussein was captured by the coalition forces, he was caught like a rat down in a hole. His days of brutality were finally over. Now don't miss this next point. Saddam Hussein has a personality style. Although I have never given him an assessment, he probably is a "*D*" type personality. He was the "Sovereign Ruler" of his country for more than 30 years. His picture and his statues were all over Iraq... until recently. Now his reign of terror has ended. Do you know who led the decision to end his "out-of-control" behavior? Another high "*D*" type personality style by the name of George W. Bush. Both men are "*D*" type personality styles. One is under control and the other was out of control. (You can figure out which is which!)

The difference between the two men is not their personality style. The difference is found in their values and character:

Hussein believes he can take someone's life whenever he wants to do so. Bush believes life is precious and should be valued at all cost.

Hussein believes in slavery, tyranny and injustice. Bush

believes in freedom, justice and the rule of law.

Hussein believes he has the final word on any issue. Bush believes the final word is "do what is right!"

The purpose of this tip is not to be political, even though I am not afraid of being political. The point is to remind each one of us to let character and integrity be the driving forces in our life, not our personality style. There are good *"Ds"* , *"Is"*, *"Ss"* and *"Cs"*. There are bad *"Ds"*, *"Is"*, *"Ss"* and *"Cs"*. Let you personality style be used for good every day of your life. Or, as Bush believes, the final word is "just do right!" Complete your personality this week with personal character and integrity. You will be glad you did!

Tip: Be character
driven, not personality driven.

Love to serve!

When I was in high school, I was invited to an "end of the year" party. One of our teachers and her husband had a group of students over to their house for a summer-time cookout.

Somehow, I got the party details mixed up. (I now see how my high "I" was working against me even back in those days - long before I understood anything about personality types!) I thought that we were asked NOT to bring a date. When I arrived, I found out that we were asked to bring a date. Everyone had a date... except me! Well, we all laughed about it. After all, it was only a cookout. It was not the end of the world.

For some reason, I decided to help the couple that was hosting the cookout. Looking back on it, I think it must have been because I was embarrassed and was trying to "save face." At any rate, I poured my heart into helping. I became the in-house waiter. I made myself a hat, put on an apron and went around the room taking orders. I cooked, served the food, poured drinks (Coke, Sprite, etc.), dipped the homemade ice-cream and then cleaned up afterwards. Actually, I was the last one to leave the party, because I was still helping.

I poured my heart into all that I did that night. No one made me do it. No one asked me to do it. For some reason, I wanted to do it... and it felt great!

When I got home late that night, my mother had already gone to bed. I went into her room to tell her about the events of the evening. I told her how good I felt inside. It was the first time that I had ever experienced anything like that. She then said to me, "Do you know why you feel so good?" I told her that I did not know.

She said, "Tonight you learned by experience one of life's greatest lessons. If you want to be great, the secret is through serving! 'Whosoever will be great among you, let him be your servant.'"* She then taught me that great leaders and great business establishments are those who have simply learned to sincerely serve many people.

Well, I never forgot that lesson. Something happened inside my heart that night. I learned the difference between "having to serve" and "wanting to serve." Oddly enough, for the next two weeks, the only thing my friends could talk about was that party and how much they enjoyed watching me be the "chief waiter."

Looking back today, I now understand the secret. Whether running a successful business, having a good marriage or leading a team at home, school, church or work, the key to success is still the same: serving with a cheerful heart. Try it this week, and watch what happens all around you, as well as inside your own heart.

Tip: Love to serve!

*Based on Matthew 20:26

6

Just do it afraid.

Fear is a strange phenomenon. There are times when fear is extremely helpful, and there are times when it is not useful at all. For example, it is extremely helpful when we are in danger from being burned by fire or when a dangerous animal is approaching.

There are many times when fear does us absolutely no good! Someone has noted that the letters F.E.A.R. could stand for False Evidence Appearing Real. This acrostic stands for the instances when fear is motivated by false danger. For example, you hear a noise just outside your home in the middle of the night, and it awakens you, but it was just the wind blowing over a trash can. Another example is the experience of feeling an airplane suddenly "drop," because it hits an air pocket, and you think it is going to crash. These are instances that contain no real need for fear, but you feel fear anyway. Wisdom is knowing when fear is useful and knowing when it is not.

I believe that fear is a type of "fuel" that moves us

through life. For the most part, it "pushes" us in a way that is hurtful and abusive. In the long run, that type of fuel wears out our human engine and defeats us. That kind of fear attacks our self-worth and keeps us from being our best.

The kind of fuel that we really need is faith. That kind of fuel tells us not to let fear get the upper hand in our life by controlling our decisions and actions.

Allow me to use a personal example. I have a lot of energy. I wake up every day wanting to learn and grow and experience new progress in my life. Ironically, I have come to see that all of that energy can very easily become a form of fear. On the other hand, I can allow that energy to become an act of faith to lead me and guide me, rather than drive me and push me. I choose to do things in faith, despite the fact that fear is still present with me in the process.

Do you remember the words from the 23rd Psalm KJV? "Yea, though I walk through the valley of the shadow of death, I will fear no evil; for thou art with me." Notice that it does not say, "I will not be afraid." Instead it says, "I will not be afraid of evil!" Fear is still present with me; I just refuse to be controlled by it! Big difference!

Fear is a necessary part of life. It is part of our make-up and being. The key is to learn to distinguish the kind of fear that is healthy versus the kind of fear that is unhealthy.

This week, begin to look past fear. You cannot make it go away, but you can refuse to allow it to control you and frustrate you. If you believe it is unhealthy fear, just ignore it, and let faith be the fuel to guide your life.

Tip: Just do it afraid.

7

The seven keys to staying young forever!

Over the years, I have heard a lot of thoughts regarding staying young. Occasionally, I have read additional ways to stay young listed in magazines, books or newspaper articles. I thought it might be a good idea to review for you these ideas. If you are already doing some of these, then good for you! If you see a couple of items that you might want to improve on, then even more "good for you!"

1. Keep learning - Be hungry to grow in your ability to acquire knowledge. Your brain is like a muscle. The more you use it, the stronger it becomes. You have heard it said, "Knowledge is power!" There is a lot of truth in that statement. I once read that the hardest thing an adult, over the age of 35, would ever learn to do is program a VCR. In my opinion, that is pitiful. We can all do better than that, but, only if we are willing to put forth the effort.

2. Keep loving - Most of us have family and friends. When

you sum up all of life, it pretty much boils down to relationships. There is a lot of energy and excitement found
in loving other people. You will find yourself thinking of
them often. Isn't it interesting that when you go on a trip,
you usually buy a gift for someone back home... someone you were thinking about... someone you love!

3. Keep laughing - (You knew that I was going to include that
one!) Laughter actually exercises your heart! Physicians are
using laughter therapy to help their patients live longer
or get well faster. The next time you are around some
children, notice how freely and openly they laugh.
When we laugh as an adult, I believe we are letting the
little boy or little girl inside of us out to play. What fun!

4. Keep laboring - Contrary to popular belief, work is not
a curse. It is a blessing. God commanded Adam and
Eve to work in their garden *before* the fall of mankind,
not simply after it. In a study done by the U.S. government concerning how long employee benefits were paid
after retirement, the results were shocking. They found
the average retired government worker lives 18 months.
That's right... only one-and-a-half years. You see, when
you have nothing to do, your body knows it, so it shuts
down... it dies! I plan on staying busy and active for a
long, long time!

5. Keep leaving - Set aside all the hurt, unfairness, injustice
and unkindness that have happened to you. Leave the
past, in the past. Learn from it; let it make you a wiser,

better person, but let it go. It will only destroy you if you choose to continue to let it eat on you.

6. Keep longing - Have dreams and goals for the future. Realize the best is still yet to come. This life is only the dress rehearsal. The real show is yet to begin! Find one area of life that needs some attention (health, finances, relationships, spiritual life, business, etc.) and look for ways you can improve that area in the future.

"Blessed are you if you are hungry in an area of life, for your longing shall be fulfilled!"

7. Keep leaning on God - Sooner or later everyone will let you down. People are human. They may mean well, but we all "flake out" from time to time. Not so with God. Even your worst day with him is better than your best day with your favorite person! It may not seem like it now, but just give it time. When you get close to stepping into eternity, you will realize that soon you will be leaning on God forever. Why not start practicing today?

Well, there they are. Why not cut these out and tape them on a 3 x 5 card and carry them around with you in your briefcase or purse? I believe if you practice these simple, seven principles, your life will be a lot better each day!

Tip: The seven keys to staying young forever!

8

Smile!

Years ago, I was in a biology class and our teacher told us that it took more facial muscles to frown then it did to smile. He explained to us that frowning caused our face to look older sooner then it normally would. Therefore, we could wear our facial muscles out by looking like a "sourpuss" all of the time. However, if we would smile a lot, we would use less muscles and cause our face to stay younger looking for a longer period of time.

I never forgot that lesson. I have always made it a habit to smile more than I frown. I am no expert on facial muscles, but I will take my biology teacher's word for it!

Recently at a function, someone handed me a poem. It meant a lot to me, and I thought I would share it with you.

A smile a day keeps troubles at bay.
It gladdens the heart of each morning you start.
Let it light up your eyes, and you'll be surprised,
At how easy it is to grin and dismiss,
To hope and believe, to build and achieve.
So for a moment a day let yourself say,
Behold...the power of a smile.

(*Rachael Mead*)

That was the original work of a young lady by the name of Rachael Mead. She wrote it after hearing me speak. She came up and told me that I had encouraged her and caused her heart to feel lighter, because she had laughed so much during my presentation. She also encouraged me by telling me that my smile was contagious and infectious.

Well, I don't know if all of that is true, but I do know that if you start smiling, it will have an impact on your own life as well as on the life of other people. In fact, I would like to challenge you to try something this week. Walk up to someone and smile real big at that person, and watch his or her face. I have been doing this lately, and I have noticed that within 3 to 5 seconds, that person smiles real big at me, and then he or she says, "What?"

Then I just look at the person and laugh, and I say, "I was wondering if my smile was contagious."

It is a proven fact that there is a direct link between our attitude and our health. Proverbs 17:22 NIV says, "A cheerful heart is good medicine." I imagine that Solomon was thinking about our smile when he wrote that verse. After all, we cannot see the heart of other people; we can only see the manifestation of their heart through their smile.

I don't know about you, but the more I smile, the better I feel. I want to encourage you to let this become an active part of your life - beginning immediately!

So this week, smile more! It will increase your face value!

Tip: Smile!

9

Learn to separate
the urgent from the important.

Years ago, I read a little booklet called Tyranny of the Urgent.[1] The author explained that each day the "urgent" things of life will be in competition with the "important" things. Urgent things are items that scream loudly at us, because they want immediate attention. Examples include: dirty dishes, paperwork, dirty clothes, tall uncut grass, computer glitches, car maintenance, deadlines at work, unpaid bills and friends with personal problems.

Important things, on the other hand, seem to be willing to take a back seat to the urgent matters. Although important things are more important than urgent things, they usually get put aside and left undone. Some important things might include: a daily quiet time, remembering someone's birthday with a card, writing a will, systematically putting money aside for retirement, going to see someone in the hospital or calling friends or family members to thank them or simply express appreciation to

46

them. It is also important to spend time with loved ones. We need to take time to take a walk with a mate or child, go to the ball game together, go out to eat, go on vacation together or turn off the telephones and watch a movie or T.V. program together.

Most of the important things in life do not scream at us. They take a back seat to the urgent things in life that do scream at us. The urgent things want immediate attention, now!

Years ago when I was a school principal, I often stayed stressed out. It seemed like I always had piles and piles of paperwork on my desk. There was no end to the paperwork! Because I felt frustrated, I sometimes was "short" when I was dealing with people or situations. One of my older, more seasoned teachers took me aside one day and said, "Just remember, paperwork has no feelings, but people do!" I never forgot that principle... Paperwork has no feelings, but people do! That was profound. It has affected me to this day. You see, I was focusing on the urgent (paperwork) rather than the important (people). Believe it or not... paperwork has no feelings, but it sure acts like it does!

Over the years, I have developed the habit of asking myself if what I am doing is urgent or important. You can do a lot of urgent things every day, and at the end of the week, you will have accomplished a lot of stuff. But, will it make any difference in the long run? On the other hand, you only need to do one or two important items, and you are well on your way to being productive and successful.

I am sure that you have heard of making a daily "to do" list. We all have created a list of items that we wanted to accomplish. The key occurs when we number our items. You see, if you have 10 items to do and you do 2-10 because they are urgent, but you leave off number 1 (the most important one), you feel empty. You feel like you failed at your plan. However, if you get number 1 done, the most important thing on your list, but you are not able to accomplish numbers 2-10, you still feel like you succeeded, because the most important thing was done.

So this week, ask yourself, "Is this item urgent or important?" Urgent items usually bear little fruit in our life. Important things usually make life worthwhile. They make life worth living. I realize the urgent things still need to be done - just don't do them, and neglect the important things in the process!

Tip: Learn to separate
the urgent from the important.

---

[1] Charles E. Hummel, *Tyranny of the Urgent!* rev. ed. (Downers Grove, Illinois: InterVarsity Press, 1994)

10

If you focus on the problem, the problem increases. If, however, you focus on the solution, the solution increases.

I have found it interesting that the more I focus my mind on things that are wrong all around me, the worse things become. However, when I try to look for the good, the pure and the positive around me, things start getting better and better. When I focus on what is good and right today, it seems I have a good, right day! But, when I focus on what is bad and wrong today, I seem to have a bad, wrong day. In other words, if I focus on the problem, the problem increases; if I focus on the solution, the solution increases.

Many of us go through life backwards. We wait until things are good to start feeling good. We wait until things are going in the right direction before we start heading in the right direction. We wait until others are doing right before we start doing right.

Do you know the difference between a thermometer and a thermostat? The thermometer adjusts itself to the temperature around itself. Whatever the temperature is, that is what the thermometer reads. A thermostat, on the other hand, sets the temperature. It is in control of its environment and makes the temperature go higher or lower as needed.

Sadly, most of us choose to be a thermometer. We wait to see how our spouse or children are behaving, and then we react accordingly. We get into traffic or go to a shopping mall and see people being rude or impatient. Then we decide how we will act. Wouldn't this week be a good time in your life to change all that? Learn to change yourself first. When I get myself under control, I am amazed at how others around me also change.

The next time that you are in an unproductive meeting that you feel is a waste of time or you are having a conversation that is going nowhere, choose to focus on the solution. Choose to be positive and upbeat. Look for anything good that you can find to do or say. Then watch what happens. Others will soon join in the new direction you set. When you become the thermostat, it does not take long before your influence is felt throughout the room. You will not only experience a difference in the environment you are in, but you will actually watch others change right before your very eyes!

We all make choices every day of our life. If I could go back and relive my life over, I would implement this tip into my life each day. Nothing is more powerful than your vision and your tongue. Work to direct your vision and your tongue this week. Look for the solutions to whatever your current challenge may be, and use your voice to speak optimistic, solution-minded words. The solutions in your life are waiting to be found. One may be just around the next corner!

Tip: If you focus on the problem, the problem increases. If, however, you focus on the solution, the solution increases.

11

Life boils down to one thing – learning to ride your bicycle!

D o you remember learning to ride a bicycle? You had seen other people do it. You knew it was possible. Yet, there was still a fear inside of you that if you tried, you might fall off. Actually, there was a good chance that you would fall off, and you knew it. Yet, there was also something inside of you that still wanted to try. You were willing to do it afraid because of one driving force inside of you, namely, you wanted to ride a bicycle!

I remember one Sunday morning, when I was very young, my mother had gone to church. My father took me outside and asked me if I wanted to learn to ride my bike without the training wheels. I immediately had two feelings . . . excitement and fear. Riding with training wheels was kind of "wobbly," but at least I knew that I was safe. Now, I was ready to grow and stretch a little. I remember asking my father, "What if I skin my knee?"

My father told me to put on a pair of blue jeans,

and then I would be okay. That did it! Now, I was ready. He held on to the back of the bike and walked along beside me a few times while I got the hang of it. I was already comfortable riding with training wheels. Now all that I needed was a little practice in learning to gain my balance. After a few tries, I took off. I remember getting all the way to the end of the circle and taking my first sharp turn. I was going a little too fast and, well you guessed it, I fell off. . . and skinned my knee. However, I was not badly hurt. Now I had gained my confidence. I was ready to get back on my bicycle and try again. Boy was my mother surprised when she came home from church!

That day, it was official. I was a full-fledged bicycle rider! And you know what? That was almost 50 years ago. . . and I can still ride a bicycle. As a matter of fact, because I learned how to do it, over the years, I have taught a lot of other people to ride a bicycle, including all four of my daughters.

I would bet my last dollar that over 99% of the people reading this tip could tell me their own bicycle-riding story. It is a common experience for all of us.

I have discovered that nearly every issue in life boils down to having the same attitude that I had when I learned to ride my bicycle. Here are my 10 truths about learning to ride a bicycle... and life:

1. This assignment is possible. Others have done it.
   I can too.

2. I feel a little fear. I will just do it afraid.
3. I know I might fall off while I am learning. That is called progress.
4. I may skin my knee, but I doubt if I will make it through life without a few bumps and bruises along the way.
5. I already have a few "training-wheel" experiences under my belt, so I am ready to take the next step on my journey.
6. I am going to do this! I am not TRYING to do this. I am in the process of actually doing this!
7. I need to work on my balance. When I am going too fast, I typically fall off. . . and skin my knee and hurt myself.
8. I need to have high expectations of myself. If I am expecting to fall off a lot, I may get what I am expecting. If I expect success, I may get that, too!
9. There will always be somebody somewhere willing to help me, and there will always be somebody somewhere surprised at my success.
10. When I learn a valuable skill, I can use it for the rest of my life, and I can share that information with others as well.

Whatever issues or challenges you are facing in life right now, I ask you to face them the same way that you did when you were young - with childlike faith. I encourage you to get on your bicycle and ride!

Tip: Life boils down to one thing – learning to ride your bicycle!

12

Whenever you feel overwhelmed, draw circles!

Over the years, I have noticed that sometimes I feel over-whelmed in my personal life. I am sure that is true of you as well. When you consider the fact that all of us wear a lot of different hats, life can sometimes be very challenging. Think about this with me just for a minute, as I explain this tip a little further.

At times, life can be frustrating due to the fact that we all have so many different areas that affect us on a daily basis. When I get completely overwhelmed, I simply get a piece of paper and pen and draw seven or eight circles. Then I will give each circle a name. For example: finances, health, children, challenge with "Joe," marriage situation, book project, upcoming trip details and responding to e-mails. When we divide our challenges, problems or situations into different categories, we are able to see them separately rather than together. At that point, we can see that our circumstances are not really quite as overwhelming as they once seemed.

I have noticed in my own experience that when I have seven or eight things that are pressing upon me, I often feel like I just cannot go on another day carrying that much "weight" on my shoulders. Haven't you felt that way? Well, I have some good news for you. First of all, God never intended any of us to carry that kind of weight. Second of all, when you divide it up into different categories, you can actually see that the problem you are having with finances, for example, is different from the fact that you need to exercise or go on a walk in order to make your body feel better.

When I give advice or counsel to someone, I frequently start by drawing circles. It helps put things in perspective. Recently, I was talking to an individual who was deeply sorrowful and depressed because of all the circumstances that had piled up at once. We divided everything into ten or eleven circles or categories. When she looked at each one of them separately, she smiled at me and said that it now feels a lot more manageable. I told her it was.

I would ask you to practice this simple technique on yourself this week. Get a piece of paper and draw seven or eight circles, and then give each circle a name. If you have more than one child, give each one of them a separate circle. What "Mary" is facing and the difficulty or frustration you are dealing with concerning her may have nothing to do with "Susie" at all. It would be a good reminder for you to separate those issues. Then list other categories that are on your mind. Putting them in separate circles will help you to back up and get a better perspective. Do not feel limited with just seven or eight circles. I have actually met some people who had to draw fifteen or twenty circles, because they had so many issues that they needed to separate. After you draw these circles, things will look more manageable, and you will be able to tackle one circle at a time.

I have seen this work for myself and others for many, many years. Why not join the team of "circle drawers" today?

Tip: Whenever you feel
overwhelmed, draw circles!

13

Have a fence - post mentality!

I never will forget the time that I built my first chain-link fence. I made it out of strong wire, and it was quite an experience.

We lived in Texas, and everyone had a fence in their backyard - everyone except us. For some reason, the people who had lived in our home before us had chosen not to have a fence. But, we had four children in our family, and we wanted the additional safety. So, I decided to put a strong chain-link, wire fence up in our backyard.

I was a school teacher at the time. One of my students, Scott Brown, told me that he and his dad had installed many fences. He said that it was pretty easy. He volunteered to help me. He told me that the key to building a good, strong fence would be in setting the fence posts correctly and securely.

Scott came over one Saturday, and we started the process. The first thing that we did was dig deep holes about every ten feet. Then we poured concrete in each hole, put the posts in the concrete and let them dry. Scott told me that it was very important to keep the posts perfectly still and secure for several days, so they would "set up" correctly. As the concrete started to settle, we adjusted the posts to be sure that they were straight. Then we left them alone to dry. Scott reminded me not to touch them, because I might break the seal at the bottom of the posts. If I did that, we would have to dig it up and start the process all over again.

The next Saturday, Scott came over to help me finish the project. The first thing he wanted to examine was the posts to see how they were doing. They were all fine. Then he did something that I will never forget. He started shaking each post back and forth with all his might! I stopped him and said, "What are you doing? You are going to mess them up!"

He laughed and said, "If these fence posts were set correctly, nothing is going to knock them down... including me!"

Recently, I was in Dallas, Texas, and I drove by our old home. Guess what? The fence is still standing strong, just like the day that we built it over 20 years ago.

Life is a lot like that fence post experience. We work as hard as we can to get stable in life by getting a good education or a good job, by getting into a good relationship or having a family or having abundant finances. Then everything in the world comes along and tries to shake us loose. Those are the tests that we all face in life.

I imagine that if a fence post had a brain, it would surely wonder, "First, you try to get me to be very still. Then, you shake the daylights out of me. Why can't you make up your mind?" But, such is the nature of this thing called life.

We should not be surprised when circumstances come to test us or shake us. No one gets through life without a few storms. The key is to remain stable during difficult times and stick to your strong foundation. Don't be surprised when you get "shook." Just stay faithful and dependable. That way you will be strong and useful for a long, long time.

Tip: Have a fence - post mentality!

14

Remember to HALT
at six specific times in your life.

About 7 years ago, I met a new friend. He was an older gentleman who spent a lot of time giving me guidance. I was going through a difficult time, and he offered me a lot of new insights out of his own personal experience. He seemed to be different from other people that I had known or been associated with in the past. He had insight and understanding and answers that really spoke to my heart.

One day I asked him where he had learned so much wisdom. He said, "Do you really want to know?" I told him that I did. The next Wednesday at 11:30 a.m., we met, and he took me to my very first A.A. meeting (Alcoholics Anonymous). I was amazed. I sat there for one hour listening to people being real and honest. It was not like anything that I had ever experienced before in my life. No one seemed embarrassed or afraid to share some of the deepest, darkest secrets of his or her life. I saw people getting free from their addictions. I saw people finding hope, strength and encouragement from other people who had walked the same path.

Needless to say, that was a turning point in my life. I continued to attend those meetings often and still do so until this day. You cannot explain A.A. You can only experience it.

In one of the meetings, I happened to notice a sign on the wall that read, "Remember to HALT." I later learned that the word "HALT" is used to remind us that there are times in all of our lives when we are more vulnerable to temptation and trouble. These times usually occur when we are Hungry, Angry, Lonely or Tired. When we going through one of those four experiences, we are usually weaker and more susceptible to stumble and fall. It is while we are in the middle of one of these warning signs that we will make our worst decisions. Those decisions are generally the ones that we will regret the most; ones that will affect our own lives and the lives of others the most.

I later learned that there are two additional S's that could make the word HALT into HALTSS. This new word adds an additional double warning to our life. The two extra S's stand for Sick and Stressed. So, there are six specific times in life to remember to HALT.

Over the past seven years, I have learned never to make an important decision when I am Hungry, Angry, Lonely, Tired, Sick or Stressed. Do you know what? My decision-making ability has greatly improved. When you put this simple tip into practice, you will begin to see remarkable results… immediately.

Life is like a game. If you play wisely and make good moves, you get good results. You win a lot. If you play recklessly or foolishly, you get bad results. You lose a lot. And nothing I know of can cause you to lose faster than making poor decisions. And poor decisions usually occur when one of the six HALTSS is disregarded.

I encourage you to create a simple 3 x 5 card motto for your desk at work or for your bathroom mirror. All it has to say is "Remember to HALT (SS) at six specific times in my life!" That will be your personal reminder to help yourself succeed in all that you do.

I have seen this simple formula save me repeatedly from making a foolish decision when a few more hours could create a completely different outlook on life.

You have heard the old saying, "You cannot turn a battleship around in five minutes." It takes time to turn anything big around and head it in a new direction. Nothing I know can help you more than this tip to understand what you are going through and when to give yourself additional time when facing those major turns in life.

Tip: Remember to HALT
at six specific times in your life.

15

Life is a process, not an event.

As I was growing up, I remember thinking to myself, "If I could just be a teenager, I would have it made!" When I became a teenager, I began to realize that it was just an event. The process of growing up continued to pass day by day.

Next, I thought, "If I could just get my driver's license, I would have it made!" When I finally got my driver's license, I began to realize it was just an event. The responsibility of driving a car, having insurance, vehicle maintenance and routine up-keep were all part of a life-long process that continued to pass day by day.

Later, I thought, "If I could just graduate from high school and go to college, I would have it made!" When I graduated from high school and went off to college, I began to realize it was just an event. The process, of figuring out how life worked, continued to pass day by day.

Next, I thought, "If I could just be married, I would

have it made!" When I got married, I began to realize that it was simply an event. The process of marriage and the major adjustments that come with that decision continued to pass day by day.

Next, I thought, "If I could just get a great job, I would have it made!" When I got a great job, I began to realize that it was just an event. The process of learning how to become skilled at my job occupied most of my daily life for years to come.

Next, I thought, "If I could just have children, I would have it made!" When I had children, I began to realize that it was simply an event. The twenty-year process of rearing children was an overwhelming responsibility that continued to pass day by day.

Next, I thought, "If I could just further my education and get advanced degrees, I would have it made!" When I received my Ph.D. degree, I began to realize that it was just an event. All I actually learned was how much there was to know and how little of it I actually knew! The dynamic of learning became a lifelong process that continued to pass day by day.

Finally, when I started my own business, I realized that I was beginning a new process. It was NOT simply an event that would happen, and then I could forget about it. I realized that I would have to work it and stick to it for years in order to see it succeed. I realized that it would be a process not an event. That was the turning point for me. I learned that an "event mentality" is short lived. A "process mentality" will help you to see the bigger picture, the long haul, the high road and the strategy that it takes to succeed.

Are you living life with an "event mentality?" Events come and go. If you start looking at things as though they are part of a process, you will be less frustrated and more patient as well as productive. A giant oak tree is beautiful; however, it did not appear as an event. It came about through a long process. That is what makes it majestic!

This week, look at everything you do through a different lens. Stop wishing your life away. See life as a process, and watch what it does to your maturity factor as well as your long-term vision.

Tip: Life is a process, not an event.

16

You learn everything by comparison or contrast.

When I was in graduate school, one of my professors asked the class an interesting question. He asked, "Have you ever wondered how we learn things?" Well, up until that time, I had not given it very much thought. After all, as long as you were learning something, what difference did it make?...so I thought.

My professor then explained to us that after we learn the basic "toddler skills" of walking and talking, we begin to learn everything by either comparison or contrast. When we learn by comparison, we learn what works and what is right and what is helpful to ourselves and to others. When we learn by contrast, we learn what is wrong and what does not work and what will hurt ourselves and others.

For example, when you learned the multiplication tables, you learned that 5 x 5 = 25. You can always count on that answer. It is right. Therefore, it becomes the standard. You can use that standard when dealing with

Robert A. Rohm Ph.D.

---

all mathematical problems. It becomes the comparison by which things are known to be right. On the other hand, have you ever touched a hot stove? It will burn you every time! You learn by contrast that you do not want to ever do that again... ever! That experience is all wrong. Contrast is a very good teacher.

When I learned the simple truth that we learn everything by either comparison (what is right) or by contrast (what is wrong), it made learning seem much simpler to me. I now look at everything I learn in one of two categories: comparison or contrast. I try to learn what is right and stick with it. When I find out what is wrong, I realize that I do not want to do that again, and I make the necessary adjustments. It makes learning simpler and life a lot easier to live.

This week, take a fresh look at your actions and behaviors. Keep doing what is right. You can measure everything by comparison with what is right. Also, avoid doing wrong. You can see the contrast of wrong actions by looking at the results they bring into your life.

Two simple words, two simple truths, two simple ways to live... and learn.

Tip: You learn everything
by comparison or contrast.

17

There is a big difference between "inspiration" and "preparation."

W hen I was growing up, I heard the words "talent," "talented" and "gifted" mentioned a lot: "He is a gifted musician. She has a lot of talent for learning languages. He is a very gifted athlete. She is a very talented student." What people were actually saying was that a person has a lot of ability in a certain area or expertise in life. I often wondered where "gifts" and "talents" were handed out. I wanted to get in that line!

There was even a T.V. show called "Talent Scout." They brought on singers, entertainers and performers in order for them to demonstrate their talent.

I realized that it is possible for someone to be born with a "bent" in a certain direction. Some people are smarter than others, some better looking, some faster and some stronger. However, the truth is that most of that is inherited from our parents in our genes. And not many of us got to choose our parents!

Over the years, I have observed that "gifts" and "talents" are very overrated. I have observed that truly great people operate on the basis of hard work, commitment and dedication.

In 1984, President Reagan was speaking to the athletes who would be representing the U.S. in the Olympic games in Los Angeles. He said to them, "Perhaps more than anyone else, ladies and gentlemen, you understand that the will to win pales in comparison with the will to prepare to win!"

What was President Reagan saying? He was referring to the thousands and thousands of hours those young men and women had spent preparing for that big moment in their life. Inspiration had been part of the work, but that paled in comparison with the preparation, hard work and dedication that each one had demonstrated in order make the Olympic team.

I believe the same is true for you and me. We may be "inspired" to do many wonderful things; however, that is usually where it ends. The decision to be faithful to the task at hand, to work hard and to be committed to our dreams or goals is another story. However, that is where true success lies!

Although I am not a "gifted" musician, I have many friends who are. They have told me that about 5% of what they do is from their "gift," and about 95% is the result of hard work. That settles the issue for me!

I challenge you to no longer look for gifts or talents

to be the way to accomplish anything in life. As the cheer-leaders in my high school said in one of their cheers, "Just buckle down, buckle down and do it, do it, do it!"

*Tip: There is a big difference
between "inspiration" and "preparation."*

You cannot truly listen as long as you want to talk!

I need to warn you right up front that this tip is not for the fainthearted. It took me over 40 years to really understand this tip and to be able to communicate it clearly to others. (I would suggest not even reading it, until you can be alone and quiet for 10 to 15 minutes.)

Communication is a major part of your life and mine. Basically, everything we do all day involves communication. Even when we are alone, we communicate with ourselves!

For many years, I believed that in order to be a good communicator, you needed to be a good talker, After all, isn't communication primarily about talking? No! It is primarily about listening... and listening involves keeping your mouth shut.

There is a two-part, secret project that you can begin to use to help you in this area. It is called being quiet and asking questions. In other words, when someone is telling you something, do not be overly eager to say something. Rather, force yourself to be quiet and listen. If you interrupt a person and begin giving your own "two cents worth" or start telling your side of the story or getting defensive, then you are sure to miss what the other person is trying to say.

Try listening to someone today and start talking each time he or she pauses. You will soon discover that you have no idea what that person is wanting to tell you. (The person may even give up and quit trying!) On the other hand, if you force yourself to wait until the person is completely finished, then ask a question about something that was just said, you will see your comprehension level increase. Ask a question that directly relates to what was just said, or ask the person to elaborate a little more about a certain point that he or she made. Then, practice the first part of the project again… be quiet.

I want to be a skilled communicator. As most of you know, that is what I do for a living. However, I am learning more and more, every day of my life, that a truly gifted communicator must first and foremost be a good listener! Every major challenge or heartache that I have faced in my life goes back to the fact that I missed something that I was being told, because my focus was on what I wanted to say back (communicate), rather than on listening to what was being said to me (communication).

Many of you have heard me refer to my Monday night men's group. I am a member of an accountability group that meets every Monday night from 7-9 p.m. I have only missed a few meetings in the last 8 years. I am amazed to see how many men have seemingly no ability to hear what is being said to them. I do not think it is simply a "male defect." (At least I hope not!) No one is born with good listening skills. They must be developed. At the beginning of the process, when one man lovingly tries to help another man see his faults or shortcomings, the response is always the same – *first defensiveness, then a lame excuse explaining how he really does not have a problem in that area of his life!* It always goes back to the same issue, namely, the inability to hear and truly receive what is actually being said.

Why do I say that this is such an important tip? Because it has the potential to make you financially prosperous. This week, when you are talking to a client or a businessperson, let him or her do the talking. That person will tell you what you need to know to close the deal if you close your mouth long enough. Ask key questions. Learn to listen to your clients - whether it is business related or family related. Learn to read your market well. If you do this, you will experience a gold mine of information and success. It is working for me... and it can work for you as well!

Tip: You cannot truly listen as long as you want to talk!

19

Do not live in regret.

L ife is a journey. It is a process. Often, we get caught in the trap of being overwhelmed with bad feelings because of things that have happened to us in the past. We find ourselves playing the "what if" game. The regret we sometimes experience feels like it will eventually crush us!

Well, I have some great news for you! We are here on this planet for about 70 years for two reasons: to learn and to grow. All of the experiences of life are to teach us about ourselves and others. God has designed it that way.

Think about it. If you could trade your life with another person, do you really believe that he or she has no challenges? Does that person have challenges with other family members or is everyone in his or her family perfect? Is that person's life free of all heartache and sorrow?

I have lived long enough to realize that if I could trade my life for someone else's, I would only be inheriting a brand-new set of problems. At the present, I am not willing to trade my set of problems for an unknown set!

Being sad and depressed will not help you. Neither will it get you to the next place you need to be. All it will do is help you to see where you failed. You must learn from your mistakes, and then ask God to begin to show you how your past mistakes can help you, as well as others, learn to do better in the future.

I believe each one of us has to come to the place where we make a conscience decision to enjoy life. If we continually think that we will be happy in life when our certain set of circumstances changes, we will never be learning the lesson life is trying to teach us today.

There will always be something trying to steal our joy. If we live in the past, we will be filled with regret and guilt. If we try to live in the future, we can be filled with fear. However, if we simply live today, knowing that today is what life is all about, then we will find peace and stability. All of life boils down to living in the present moment. Do not waste your "right now" hoping for something better in the future.

Someone wisely once noted, "You cannot enjoy life if you do not enjoy yourself." It has taken me a long time to realize that we are all human. We all make mistakes. Learning to laugh at ourselves as we learn and grow makes life a lot easier to handle. If we are not careful, we can focus on regret and our own past failures until it makes us physically and emotionally sick. God guarantees forgiveness and a new start every day of our lives. If he does not want me to live in regret, why should I?

Tip: Do not live in regret.

20

When working with others, be sure to include both the big idea and the details.

When I was in the sixth grade, we were allowed to choose which musical instrument we wanted to learn to play. I will never forget the day that Mr. Bradley, the high school band director, came to visit our elementary school. All of the sixth graders got to go into the school auditorium. We were shown all of the different instruments. Mr. Bradley demonstrated how each instrument worked. (He could play every one of them. I was very impressed!) We were then allowed to choose the one instrument that we wanted to learn to play. As I now look back on all of this, I realize that this process could not have been more random!

I chose the trumpet, because it was loud and shiny! We then were allowed to rent the instrument from our local music store for 3 months, so that Mr. Bradley could begin to give us music lessons. He would come by our school once each week for the next 3 months to teach us. The following fall, we would be going into the 7th grade, and we would be in the band. It was all so exciting.

I remember my first lesson. It was hard, and I was confused. I did not understand the concepts of practice, self-discipline, consistency, hard work or focus. I did understand loud and shiny! I lasted the 3-month trial period; then, I turned in my trumpet. I did not like the experience. I still suffer from a bad attitude toward the trumpet to this very day! (I now realize that I would have enjoyed playing the drums! But, that is another story!)

Over the next 6 years, many of my friends learned how to play their musical instrument. They ended up in the marching band. I, however, went the route of athletics and enjoyed that very much. Consequently, the only musical instrument that I know how to play today is the radio!

Now that I am an adult, I have made a wonderful discovery. When you are working with people who have a different mind-set than you do, it is important to discuss both the big idea as well as the details. Mr. Bradley focused on the big idea. ("You can be in the band!") However, he did not mention any of the details in his presentation. ("You are not going to automatically know how to play your instrument. It takes time and practice every day, but eventually, you will catch on to it.") Giving these details would have been helpful.

The Ford Edsel automobile failed because of a lack of a clear idea about the big picture. Ford covered the details. The Edsel actually was a highly proficient automobile. Many are still in good condition to this very day. However, Ford failed in the big idea category, because the general public did not know the target market that the Edsel was designed to reach. Was it for the rich, middle class or poor? Was it better than a Cadillac? Was it worse than a Chevrolet? No one knew. So, no one bought it. No one had the big idea!

Recently, I did a presentation for a company. I had the details, but I failed to have a clear picture of the big idea in my head. Consequently, I missed the mark in my training program. They were disappointed. After I realized what happened, I was disappointed. I will not let that happen again. I created a new check sheet for myself. It has 2 major points on it. I have discovered those two concepts are very different.

1. What materials or details or specifics do I want to cover?
2. What is the big idea that I want to accomplish?

This week, take a closer look at both the big idea and the details in something that you are doing. Keep them separate as you prepare or review your work. It will help you separate issues better, as well as help other people know what is going on!

If you work at this, who knows, one day you may be able to blow your own horn!

Tip: When working with others, be sure to include both the big idea and the details.

21

Greatness is on the
other side of submission.

R ecently, I was talking to my good friend Pete Hinojosa. Many people have heard me refer to Pete as one of the most outstanding school teachers in America. He lives in Houston, Texas and works with the Spring Branch Independent School District. He is a high *"D/I"* personality style. I have watched his work grow over the years, and believe me, in time you will be hearing great things from Pete.

Like most of us, Pete has one area of his life in which he has had to grow. It is the area of being under authority. Can anyone identify with that? None of us by nature likes being told what to do. I remember when I was talking to one of my children years ago. She was having a very difficult day. I asked her, "Why won't you do what you were told to do?"

She looked at me and said, "I just obeys myself!"

Well, as you can imagine, we had to work our way through that situation! But, I couldn't help but laugh on the inside as I thought to myself, "Yes, you are part of the fallen human race of which we are all members. We all have the attitude, 'I just obeys myself!' "

Over the years, Pete has learned to keep the dominant part of his personality under authority to those whom he serves. It is through that simple truth that more and more greatness has entered his life.

Many of you have heard the secret tip that we use for this particular personality type. For the high *"D"* (Dominate Type), we always say, "Before you can be IN authority, you must learn to be UNDER authority." Every person who achieved greatness in his or her life, and who was helpful to other people, has done so by following this simple truth. No one is an island unto himself or herself. No one can go through life without having someone being an authority over him or her. The only person in the universe who is not under someone else's authority is God himself. Therefore, doesn't it make sense that He is the ultimate authority to whom we must all bow?

This week, let me encourage you not to fight or resist the authority under whom you now serve. Whether it is a teacher, parent, husband, wife, employer, police officer, military officer or someone else, realize that their position of authority brings with it a degree of respect. I will be the first to recognize that not everyone in authority always exercises or uses his or her authority correctly, but that is not the point. We can all look for loopholes all day long, but when we are finished looking for excuses, we still must learn that success is found by cooperation and obedience, not by rebellion and disobedience.

Look for ways this week that you can be more cooperative to the authorities that are over you. God promises that he has a special blessing for all those who are wise enough to follow that path.

Tip: Greatness is on
the other side of submission.

22

Be sure to grow wiser as you grow older.

This week I will celebrate another birthday. They still seem to come up at least once every year! I am grateful for many things – a wonderful country, good health, four grown daughters, two great son-in-laws, two precious grandsons, a fabulous staff, a growing business... well, you get the idea. I could go on and on. Again, I am very grateful for so many things.

Perhaps the one thing I am most grateful for this year is wisdom. I was taught a long time ago that we grow older with each passing year; however, growing older does not guarantee that we are growing wiser. We get older every year, but, it is possible to stay immature forever!

Years ago, I was on a church staff in Dallas, Texas. One day, I was talking to a fellow staff member. He had been on the church staff about ten years, which was a lot longer than me. He gave me a lot of good, helpful information that day. Perhaps the most important thing he taught me was to learn from the past mistakes of others. He said,

"Hopefully I have learned at least one important lesson from being on this mega-church staff over these past ten years: There is a big difference between working somewhere ten years or working there ONE year TEN times!"

That was one of the most profound things I had ever heard! Through the years, I have seen that concept apply over and over to a variety of people and situations. Just because you are in a particular set of circumstances does not mean you are actually learning and growing in that environment. How many people do you know who have been married for ten years... when actually they have only been married for ONE year, TEN times!

Unless you are really committed to growing wiser with each passing day of your life (learning from your mistakes and trying to do better in different areas of life), you will only grow older with each passing year. Growing older is not a guarantee that you are gaining any wisdom from life. You must seek for it, desire it, look for it and want it. Otherwise you will simply grow older, but stay immature forever.

This week look for ways to learn from your past mistakes or the mistakes of others. Actually put forth some effort to see how to make a difficult situation a little better. Maybe things cannot change overnight. But, they will never change unless you learn and grow from the lessons life is trying to teach you. After all... who wants to learn ONE year's worth of lessons TEN times? Wouldn't ten years of lessons in ten years be a lot better? I believe it would!

Tip: Be sure to grow wiser as you grow older.

23

I think I am right, but I may be wrong.

Have you ever worked with a "know-it-all?" It is difficult at best. I believe, at times, we ourselves become that "know-it-all" person. Often we find ourselves in a situation where it is very important that the information we are acting upon is correct. Once we believe we are right, off we go! We pay little attention to the fact that it is far better to double check than to be in a hurry.

We have all experienced getting lost on a road trip. We did not intend to get lost. We thought that we were headed in the right direction. At the time, we thought we were right, but we turned out to be wrong.

Recently, in the news, we have been told that President Bush was given some bad information by the CIA. Immediately, everyone's attention focused on the CIA. Why? It was because no one can possibly know everything. All of us, including the President of the United States, have to rely on others to communicate in a manner that will help us to be in a position to make the best decisions possible each day.

When someone gives you inaccurate information, no one faults you for your poor decision. After all, you were acting in good faith based on the facts as best you knew them at the time. However, it is up to you to do your own homework. You might think you are right, but double-checking yourself may prevent you from being wrong!

A few months ago, I was talking to a friend of mine who is a dentist. He was telling me that he had lost a lot of money in both Enron and Worldcom. He went on to say, "I did not allow myself to feel too badly about it, because I did not know that I was dealing with dishonest numbers. If I had known the truth, I would have made better choices." He thought he was right. It turned out that he was wrong.

As I reflected on his comments, I asked myself a hard question, "How many things do I think are really right in my life, yet they may be wrong?" It is one thing to simply make a wrong turn while driving or lose some money in the stock market. Those things are unfortunate but certainly not life shattering! However, in other areas of life, we need to be very careful. Examples are: choosing your life marriage partner, selecting your chosen life's vocation, correctly developing your relationship to God, planning for your retirement years, wisely choosing what foods you put into the only body that you will ever have and rightly guiding or correctly rearing your children. You get the idea.

The older I get, the more I see how important it is to

make wise decisions. I have learned to approach decision making with a whole new attitude. "I think I am right, but I may be wrong." That simple truth has done wonders for my insights. It has taken the pressure off me from having to BE right and shifted it to being open to what IS right!

The next time you make a decision, approach it with the new attitude, "I think I am right, but I may be wrong." You will not only feel differently about the decision-making process, but you will think twice before you move ahead in your decision. It is freeing and healthy. Try it this week. Once you experience it, you will approach decisions in a whole new manner.

Tip: I think I am right, but I may be wrong.

24

Are you trying to win,
or are you trying not to lose?

During my senior year at Griffin High School, we had a great football team. Most of us had played together since we were in grammar school. We were blessed with a lot of talent, even though we were only a small town located 40 miles south of Atlanta.

Our football team had won nearly every game that we played that year and now we were facing our biggest test, Southwest High School from Atlanta! They were big, fast and fearsome. They had three of the best players in the state of Georgia on their team. (All three would later go on to become starters on college football teams.)

The first half of the game was all ours. We seemingly could do nothing wrong, and they seemingly could do nothing right. At the halftime, we were ahead 13-6. We went into the dressing room fired up!

After we all had some water and calmed down a little bit, our coach spoke to us. He told us that we were playing great! He told us how proud he was of all of us. He said that he knew this game was ours!

Then it happened! If I live to be 100 years old, I will never forget what he said next. "Okay, boys, now in the second half, we are going to play some conservative football!"

I had no idea what he was saying that night. I was only 17 years old at that time. I had no frame of reference by which to measure what he was saying to us. I later found out what he meant. What he was trying to tell us was that we were going to try to hold on to our lead. We were not going to try to win. We were going to try not to lose! (Even as I write this, I still feel a sick feeling in the pit of my stomach!)

We went back out on the field and played conservative football. We did not try to score another point. All we did was try to keep them from scoring. We did a pretty good job, but the wind had been taken out of our sails. We felt whipped. We were able to hold them to one more touchdown and extra point. The game ended in a 13-13 tie. That was the turning point in our season. The one team, Robert E. Lee High School, who had defeated Southwest High School, got to go to the state play-offs. It should have been us, from Griffin High School, because we had the best overall record. But, Robert E. Lee High School had beaten Southwest High School, and our game with them had ended in a tie.

I remember that there was a lot of "stink" that

occurred among the fans. The coach lost his coaching job. He was "promoted" to administration. Over the years, I heard it was because of his decision to try to play "conservative football."

Today, looking back, I am grateful for that experience. It taught me a lot. I have come to understand an important truth. When you are not afraid to lose, you are going to win! If we had gone back on the field and kept our momentum going, we would have won the game. I am sure of it. We would have gone to the state play-offs, and who knows where from there.

I have seen it in business, ministry, relationships, education, finances and on and on. When you give anything your best try with all your heart, to the very end, you will come out far better than if you simply try to hold on to the little bit you have.

In a survey taken of senior adults, when asked what they wish they had done differently in their life, the answer came back over and over again - taken more risks.

I am not recommending that you go to Las Vegas and put all your savings on the table. But neither am I recommending that you put it all in a mattress and save it for your retirement!

My mistakes and failures are making my life an exciting adventure. I may fail. I may lose. I may be defeated! But, I know one thing for sure - I am going to give life all I have! I am not going to try to keep from losing. I know how that feels. I tried that in the fall of 1966, and it ended up in a tie! I don't want to do that again. I am going to try to win. I am shooting for the moon... and even if I miss, I will end up somewhere in the stars! I'll see you there!

Tip: Are you trying to win,
or are you trying not to lose?

25

Sometimes things are not as easy as they look!

Recently I was taking a flight from Atlanta, Georgia to Dallas, Texas. I was sitting on the airplane and watching other passengers as they boarded. One by one they passed me and headed down the aisle to take their seat. All of a sudden, I noticed a very large individual trying to get down the aisle. She had a small child with her, and she was carrying a couple of large carry-on bags. The child was pulling a rolling cart, and they were having some major challenges. If you have ever been on an airplane, you know the aisles are not very accommodating. When you have a lot of large bags with you, as well as being very large yourself, it is going to be a very uncomfortable situation.

Anyway, as they passed by, I slid over to try to give them a little more aisle space. Their seats were a couple of rows behind me and off to my left. As they tried to store their luggage, they found that it would not fit in any of the overhead compartments, because it was simply too large. In the meantime, the line behind them had come to a complete halt. The lady and her son were blocking everyone in the entire aisle and keeping other passengers from getting to their seat. The flight attendant did everything in her power to help both of them, but things were getting worse by the second. After she took their bags to try and find a place for them in the back of the plane, it was time for the woman and her child to take their seats. That was another challenging situation. The woman actually needed two seats because of her physical size. (I am in no way being unkind or critical about her situation. I am just telling you what I observed.)

After the lady and her son were seated, the people who had been standing in line for a long time trying to get past them were finally able to move down the aisle. I noticed a gentleman about three or four people back that was very well dressed and looked very distinguished. As he slowly walked by me, I reached out and gently grabbed his arm and motioned for him to lean over to me. He looked at me and leaned down closer to my head. I whispered to him, "Sir, I have been watching you as you stood there and allowed the lady and her son and all their luggage to get situated. That was one of the finest displays of patience that I have ever seen in my life."

He looked at me, smiled, and softly said, "It was not as easy as it looked!" We both got a chuckle out of his comment to me.

As he walked down the aisle, I thought to myself, how true it is that most of the difficult things in life that we do with a good attitude are not as easy as they look. Most of us would be much happier if we could openly gripe, complain, whine, moan, and groan about everything that happens in our life that does not suit us. But, sometimes it is better to simply look at the bright side of a situation and do all we can to make the best of a difficult set of circumstances.

This week, let me encourage you to keep a good, positive attitude regardless of who is currently "blocking your aisle!" It may be difficult, but no one said that everything in life would be easy! Remind yourself that other people may be observing you. It may be difficult on the inside of you, but outwardly, take the high road and do all you can to make it look easy. You will be a blessing to someone who is watching you...just like the man on the plane was to me!

Tip: Sometimes things are not as easy as they look!

26

You have to do your job and everyone else's, too!

This tip can be easily misunderstood. It may sound negative or cynical. However, it is not meant to be perceived in that light. Rather, it is meant to be a helpful word of instruction to teach you how to head things off before you get ambushed!

In order to get through life, we must realize that no one can do everything. We all have to rely on other people in almost every endeavor of life. We must rely on mechanics to repair our vehicles, restaurant servers to get our order right and we must have other co-workers to help carry out daily responsibilities. And therein lies the challenge. If you really want something done correctly - exactly like you want it done - then you have to operate with the attitude that says, "I have to do my job and everyone else's, too."

Have you ever placed an order at a drive-through window at a fast-food restaurant? If your attitude was, "I will place my order, and they will get it right," then you are not thinking correctly... especially if you want your order to be right! However, if your attitude was, "I will place my order, and I sure hope they get it right... but, even if they don't, that's okay, because I am going to double check it – then you realize that you have to do your job and everyone else's, too!" Now that is correct thinking.

I can hear some of you saying, "Dr. Rohm, that is the most ridiculous thing that I have ever heard. If they can't get my order right, they shouldn't be working there in the first place!"

I agree with you, but let me ask you a question, "Why are you willing to let the inefficiency, immaturity and inexperience of another person control your life?"

This week I was in an office supply store. I had a coupon for some paper. The coupon offered 50% off each box with a maximum purchase of 3 boxes. The cashier rang up 3 boxes of paper, but only scanned in the coupon one time. So, my receipt showed the discount on only one box of paper. I politely showed the cashier that he needed to scan the coupon two more times in order to make the transaction correct. After I explained to him how to do it, he looked at me and said, "We make a good team!"

I thought to myself, "That is because I realize that I have to do my job and everyone else's, too!"

Now don't miss this next point - I know it was his job to get it right, but it was my transaction and my purchase and my money and my responsibility to see to it that it was all done correctly. I was not expecting him to get it right, so I was able to maintain my alertness. If you want to grow, you have to begin to be aware of things and see things that others simply do not see or are not even aware of.

If you ask my staff members, they will tell you that this tip has helped them over and over again. It becomes a mind-set. It becomes a way of life! You start thinking in terms of personal responsibility instead of blame. You become more proactive rather than reactive. You learn to see things more clearly. You begin to become more alert to the possibility of what could potentially destroy your dream!

Recently, I started working with a new publisher. They faxed me a credit application. I filled it out and returned it to the publisher. A few days later, my bank called me to ask if it was all right to send the publisher the requested financial information. I gave my approval. Then, a few days later, the publisher called me wanting to know when the credit application would be returned to them in order for them to process the application. I explained to them the fact that my bank had already contacted me about their request. I asked them why they thought my bank would be calling me if they (the publisher) had not yet received my paperwork. There was a long pause of silence on the other end. A few minutes later, they e-mailed me stating that everything was in order. (It makes me wonder if I am using the right publisher on this project. Hopefully the press people check things more closely than the business office!)

I realize that you can drive yourself crazy utilizing this tip. But, I also know that I am talking about an attitude and a philosophy of life not a concrete rule or law.

I have one more story to share. This morning I was in a coffee shop. I ordered a large coffee. I did not pay attention to the size of the cup that the person behind the counter picked up. When they handed me my coffee, I noticed it was a medium, not a large. I ask the attendant, "Is this the large size?"

She looked at me and said, "Oh, I gave you the medium by mistake."

I told her that it was okay; the medium was fine. Then I thought to myself, "I failed to practice my own tip: You have to do your job and everyone else's, too!"

This week, start practicing this tip. Then when something goes astray, you will not be shocked. Instead, you will be prepared to deal with it, because you are alert.

The key to great vision is being ahead of the possibilities that life deals you and responding in a healthy, proactive manner. This is wisdom at its best!

*Tip: You have to do your
job and everyone else's, too!*

27

If you tell the truth, you never have to remember what you said.

H ave you ever caught someone in a lie? Have you ever lied yourself and were caught? We could all probably answer *yes* to both questions.

Sometime in the past, you learned that lying is definitely not the way to go. I guess God knew that, too. After all, the issue of lying did make the top 10 list, "Thou shalt not bear false witness."

When I was growing up my father often made this statement to me, "If you tell the truth, you never have to remember what you said!" I did not understand at first, what he meant. Why would I try to memorize everything I said? It took me a little while for it to sink in.

When I tell the truth, I simply have to tell what actually happened from my perspective. My own thoughts, recollections, experiences and feelings come from within me. I usually spend a lot of time with myself. (So far, 55 years!) Have you ever noticed, wherever you go, there you are! When you tell the truth about an event or an experience, you do not have to remember what you said, because you are simply recounting the truth. A few weeks from now when you tell the same information again, it will remain the same, because that is what happened. Your mind easily finds the same truthful information to repeat whenever you need to repeat it, because that is the way the mind works. It remembers the truth.

A lie is not like that. You tell some false information today and two weeks from now, you cannot remember what you said. Then you have to tell another lie to cover up the first one. Then two weeks later, you find you are in even deeper water. It will not be long until you start to drown. No one has the mental capacity to remember every lie that he or she has told. Yet, all of us do have the mental capacity to remember the truth... without ever trying to memorize what we said.

I am often asked how I can remember so many stories about my life or events that have happened to my family or friends. Actually, it is easy. I have not tried to remember or memorize anything. I simply recount what took place at the time from my perspective. Because I tell what happened, I do not have to memorize it. My mind will do that for me. If I am lying, the next time I tell the story, it will be different and confusing... and people will notice. Eventually, someone will say something. Things just will not add up!

Why do you think, in a court of law, a person is cross-examined? Both sides want to hear everything, from every angle. If you tell the truth... no problem. If you lie... good luck... you will need it!

This week, tell the truth. When you live openly and aboveboard, your mind will help you remember everything you need to know to make this journey called "life" a success!

Tip: If you tell the truth, you
never have to remember what you said.

28

It is more important to admit your mistakes than it is to keep people from thinking you were wrong.

T his week's tip will require a little bit of thought...and humility. I have discovered that from time to time every one of us can use a good dose of humility, even though it is sometimes hard to swallow.

A friend of mine once told me, "It is not the fact that all of us make mistakes that really matters. What really matters is what people do about their mistake once they see it." I believe this is really true.

Have you ever stopped and wondered why it is so hard and difficult to admit it when you are wrong? I think at the root of it is human pride. None of us wants to admit that we were wrong or that we made a mistake. Sometimes it is because we do not want to be embarrassed. Other times it may be because we do not want to lose our popularity. For some of us, it is simply because we do not want to admit that we could possibly be wrong!

The truth of the matter is that we all make mistakes.

Welcome to the human race! A long time ago, I heard that there are a few short sentences that every one of us should memorize and learn to use on a daily basis:

- The five-word version is, "I won't do that again."
- The four-word version is, "It was my fault."
- The three-word version is, "I was wrong."
- The two-word version is, "I'm sorry." (Or in today's lingo… "My bad.")
- The one-word version is, "Ooops!"

Why not try to incorporate those five simple sentences in a lot of your communication this week. I have watched the positive results time and time again when I use these simple words in my own life.

For those of you who are old enough to remember Richard Nixon and the Watergate situation, you may have noticed that history has proven to be very hard on President Nixon. However, everyone pretty much agrees that if Nixon had come out on the first day of the Watergate scandal, and publicly stated, "This was wrong; we made a mistake. I take full responsibility for this action, and it will never happen again," the American public would probably have forgiven him.

There's just something inside every one of us that demonstrates mercy when a person makes a mistake, and is willing to own up to it. Likewise, there is something in all of us that despises someone who will not admit his or her own faults. Solomon, the wisest man who ever lived, said in Proverbs 28:13 NIV, "He who conceals his sins does not prosper, but whoever confesses and renounces them finds mercy."

This tip isn't easy to read, but it is very important that we all learn to practice this tip. I know that every time I have done this, it has made me a better person, and it will you, too.

Tip: It is more important
to admit your mistakes than it is
to keep people from thinking you were wrong.

29

When you demonstrate organization, you are actually making a statement.

We all live in a very busy world. Every day of our life, we all have a lot of activities going on. For example, if you have a vehicle or a home, just taking care of routine maintenance can easily become a full-time assignment. It is easy to let a lot of things "slide," because trying to keep up with boring, routine, mundane matters can be time consuming, not to mention a lot of "out go" with very little "income" in return. Trying to stay "on top of things" can become very wearisome indeed.

I have observed something that is making many businesses (and individuals) very wealthy. It is called organization. You see, when you are organized, you are actually making an important statement to your clients and friends. You are saying, "I believe this information is important; therefore, I have spent a major investment of time, effort, energy and expense to make it useful, practical and helpful for others to enjoy."

Think about this thought for just a second: How much

money is spent daily on T.V. or newspaper ads? Millions! And, the more clear or organized or user friendly a company becomes, the more revenues they will generate.

If companies or individuals are unclear and unorganized, it communicates a message loud and clear, "Warning, we do not know what we are doing, so please do not do business with us. We will only frustrate and confuse you!"

How many times have I been asked to "click here" for further information, only to be taken to a notice that states, "Web site does not exist." We, at Personality Insights, Inc., have done it, too! So I am not talking about perfection. I am talking about organization.

When you get organized, you are actually saying, "I have thought this out, and I want to make this experience good for you and not confusing. This information or product is worthy of your attention and respect, so I have tried to be clear in order not to frustrate you." See what I mean?

This week, raise your organizational skills. No one naturally fully excels in this area. We all can do better. The more organized you are, the less frustrated you will be. The more organized you help others become, the more productive they will be. It requires a lot of time, effort, energy and thought, but it is well worth it. The more you practice it, the more you see it. I promise!

Tip: When you demonstrate organization, you are actually making a statement.

30

Disappointment will not kill you!

Have you ever been anxious for something to happen, but regardless of how hard you tried, you just could not seem to make it happen? We all have had that experience. We slowly began to wake up to the realization that some things are simply beyond our own control. It may be something as simple as the weather. For example, we had a trip planned and wanted pretty weather, but it rained. At other times, it may be more serious. For example, we wanted a relationship to work out, but the other person did not. Therefore, we end up hurt or disappointed.

I have discovered that disappointment is in my life for a reason. It is an excellent teacher that helps me follow the right path in life. It provides great lessons on how to do things better in the future. It teaches me that if I do things differently next time, I may get different results next time. Yes, disappointment is a reality of life, and all of us have experienced it from time to time.

The real challenge comes into our life when we no longer want to try things, because we are afraid we may get disappointed. But remember, disappointment is not meant to be an enemy, but a friend... to help instruct us.

When we were children, we tried new things, because we had more confidence. We had not yet experienced the cruel feelings of disappointment. As we got older, we began to experience the hurt and pain that would often accompany disappointment. So, in time, we quit trying. Rather than actually living life, we began to sit back and just let life happen. We moved from being a participant to being a spectator.

This week, I want to ask you to consider getting back into the game. Start to reengage in life even if you might end up getting disappointed again! It does not cost you anything to hope and believe for a good outcome in the future. The only price you could possibly pay is that you might believe for something and then end up getting disappointed. But, think about the alternative... if you do not believe for something, you are sure to be disappointed! Faith will help you and me to begin to walk through all of our disappointments. Faith is actually preparation for disappointment!

One last thing, I have learned is that there is a big difference between anticipating disappointment and actually being disappointed. It turns out that what we often anticipate happening is actually a lot worse than what ends up happening. But again, we won't know what will happen until we try.

Anticipating disappointment hurts a lot more that actually being disappointed. That is because the fear of disappointment is so strong. And that is because it is in the future not simply in the past.

Faith calls us to try and try, then try again, as we walk into the future. That is why, in reality, successful people are really failures who just kept trying. No one gets it right on the first try... or the second or the third! We need to walk into the possibility of our success or disappointment rather than run from it.

Life is full of all kinds of emotions and feelings and experiences. Disappointment is simply one of them to help us arrive safely at our final destination. Stay on the journey!

Tip: Disappointment will not kill you!

31

Be a fish!

hen I was growing up, my father would often say to me, "Be a fish!" I would wonder what he meant by that statement. Not understanding anything about personalities at the time (and being an out-of-control high "*I*" type), I would often talk more than I would listen. And that is when I would hear, "Robert, you know what? You would be a lot better off if you would learn to be more like a fish!"

One day, I asked my father, "What does it mean to be a fish?"

He laughed and said to me, "As much as you talk, I was wondering when you were going to ask me about that!" Then he simply said, "A fish would not have problems if he could just learn to keep his mouth shut!"

Although I did not catch on immediately, it slowly began to sink in. Sometimes it is better not to say anything. Every personality style can potentially struggle with this tip, but none more so than the high "*I*" type.

Just because you have something to say, does not mean that you have to say it. I am still learning that it is very difficult to be a good listener if all you are thinking about is what you are going to say the next time there is a "lull" in the conversation. Besides, if you learn to keep your mouth shut, no one can accuse you of being unkind or a smart aleck or worse yet, stupid!

The wisest man who ever lived, Solomon, put it this way in Proverbs 17:28 NIV, "Even a fool is thought wise if he keeps silent and discerning if he holds his tongue."

In business, we are taught not to overstate our case. We can sell our clients, and then talk them out of the purchase! In other words, this all requires practice, patience and balance. I have discovered that it is not easy to be a fish. It is a lifelong pursuit. I hope you are in the process of working on this worthy project.

Tip: Be a fish!

32

Personal growth is simply learning to do the things that you do not want to do.

Have you ever had something to do that you simply did not want to do? Have you ever gone ahead and done it anyway? How did that make you feel? Well, I think I know the answer to that question. It made you feel great! Why? Because a big part of personal growth and development is learning to simply go ahead and do the things that you sometimes do not want to do.

After I graduated from high school, I spent the next two years of my life in a military environment. I attended Gordon Military College. Talk about a shock to my system! They told me when to get up, when to eat, when to go to class, how to dress, when to study, how to walk correctly, when to go to the bathroom, how to fold my clothes and when to go to bed! Up until that time, I had pretty much done all of those activities the way and the time that was most convenient to me. (And "most convenient" meant that frequently they never were done!)

Over the years, I have come to see the power in routine, living on purpose, knowing how to say *no* to my own laziness, learning how to stay focused and creating some self - discipline in my own life. Living in that manner creates better results than simply drifting through life like a tumbleweed.

I have oftentimes heard the expression, "We need to move to a whole new level!" You probably have heard someone say that as well. Have you ever wondered exactly what that means? For me, it simply boils down to learning to do things I do not want to do or learning to do things that I do not currently know how to do. Those things can be uncomfortable for me... just like military school; however, the fruit and benefits are too good to pass up.

This week, why not take a look at something that has been hanging over you for a long time. Maybe it is cleaning out the garage or starting an exercise program. Maybe it is simply writing a thank-you note or a letter to a friend. It could be as serious as writing a will just in case something happens. It may feel uncomfortable at first, but as any pilot will tell you, the hardest part of the flight is getting the plane off the ground!

Ladies and Gentlemen... prepare for take off!

Tip: Personal growth is simply learning to do the things that you do not want to do.

33

Uncover your motives - you may not like what you find, but your motives are the key to your personal growth.

T his tip is difficult. I do not like it. You may not like it either! It is very painful. But, as the saying goes...
"No pain, no gain!"

Do you know why you often do the things you do? When was the last time that you asked yourself that question? Allow me to relate a story to you.

Recently, I was having lunch with a group of people. When the food came, one of the men at the table immediately and abruptly said to the rest of us, "Let's take a moment to thank God for our food and ask the blessing!" He looked at me and said, "You pray!" I did so, and we all started enjoying our lunch together.

I thought to myself, "It was nice to see how focused that man was on thanking God for our food!"

Later the next night, I was talking to his wife. It was a casual conversation about general information. Suddenly, she changed the conversation and asked me a question. "Did you see how focused my husband was on quickly saying the blessing when the food arrived at the table?"

"Yes, that impressed me very much!"

She then said, "That had nothing to do with the blessing!"

"It didn't?" I responded.

"No, he simply likes to eat his food when it is real hot!"

That conversation made me feel uncomfortable for several reasons. First, I do not believe that it is right to listen to someone tell me about his or her marriage partner's faults. Secondly, I do not believe it is my place to try to straighten out a situation when no one has asked for my advice. Thirdly, I began to feel disappointed as I reflected back on the whole "lunch blessing" incident.

Later that evening, I was feeling a little sad. I started to wonder if my motive for "asking a blessing" at mealtime was because I really wanted to thank God for his provision in my life or just because I was in a hurry to eat. I said a little prayer and asked God to help me to check my motives in the future. I even told God that I would rather eat cold food with a truly grateful heart, than eat hot food simply because I was focused on meeting my own wants.

See, I told you this tip was difficult! This week, ask yourself why you do the things you do. Also, ask a close friend to tell you if he or she feels or senses something odd about the way you do a certain thing.

The real tragedy in the above story is that this woman does not feel the freedom to talk to her own husband about something that she considers serious and important. If it were you, do you think you would receive her comments openly and be willing to change the way you "do the blessing," or would you simply feel resentment at being told the truth about something to which you are somewhat blind?

Growth is sometimes painful... but it is very, very valuable. It is very valuable indeed.

Tip: Uncover your motives - you may not like what you find, but your motives are the key to your personal growth.

34

Failure is an event, not a person.

We live in a confusing world. We are taught from a very young age that failure is a bad thing... and it is! Unfortunately, we are not taught to separate failure (as an event) from our own personhood. No one will make it through life without failing in some endeavor from time to time. The key is to recognize the fact that we may have failed at some event, but we are not a failure as a person, in and of ourselves.

In 1991, I started my own business, Personality Insights, Inc. At the time, I had another job, but I wanted to work for myself. One day, I was looking at my calendar, and I noticed that I had 23 small speaking engagements lined up. Most of them were "freebies," and the ones that were paying me did not amount to very much. Suddenly, the thought crossed my mind, "I wonder if I could do this on a full-time basis? I wonder if I could make a living by doing something I really love?"

At that time, I carried a 3 x 5 card in my wallet with three quotes written on it that I often read. I pulled the card out of my wallet and began reading:

1) Failure is the opportunity to begin again more wisely.
2) Obstacles are those frightful things that you see when you take your eyes off your goals.
3) Failure is an event, not a person.

The third quote seemed to shout at me! Suddenly, I realized that I might fail at my new endeavor, but that would be okay. For the first time in my life, I felt free about failing, if it happened. I knew that I could fail working for myself as easily as I could fail while I was working for another person or organization. If I failed, it would simply be an event in my life; it would not be me as a person. It was time to take the step!

Now, 12 years later, I can hardly believe I waited so long to take that step. I wish I had done it 20 years earlier... but I was not ready at that time. These past 12 years have been the most rewarding, most difficult, most exciting, most nerve-racking, most adventurous years of my life. I would not trade what I have learned from going through all those experiences for anything! And you know when it all started? The day I awakened to the fact that failure is an event, not a person.

What are you wrestling with in your life right now? What do you know is the next right thing you need to face?

Do you feel that you will be a failure if you try something you are currently only dreaming about? Well, this tip could be just what the doctor ordered to remind you that it may be time to attempt to start living your dream. Even if you fail, you will be proud of yourself for making the effort. Besides, you might succeed.

Tip: Failure is an event, not a person.

35

Wherever you are, be all there!

We live in a very fast-paced world. Everything is "instant"... from coffee to food to travel. We grew up watching T.V. programs that taught us that most relationship problems could be resolved in about 30 minutes. Now, even the most difficult, complex legal cases on "Law and Order" can be resolved in one hour!

Many times that mind-set causes us to be in one place physically but another place mentally. Think about it. How many times have you been with someone, and he or she looked at you and said, "Where are you? What were you thinking about?"

Then you "snapped back" into reality and said, "Oh, nothing... I was just daydreaming."

Actually, this can even happen when you are alone. You can be working on your computer and a thought comes floating along through your mind and off you go... to somewhere else.

Some of these experiences are normal and even healthy. After all, unless we dream, we will never grow beyond our present set of circumstances. However, what I am talking about is learning to focus: be where you are and be committed to the task at hand - the one in front of you at this moment.

I was in military school my first 2 years of college. What a shock! They told us when to get up, when to eat, when to go to class, when to study, when to march, how to dress and when to go to bed. They even told us when we could go to the bathroom!

During my first year, I could not wait to get out of there. By my second year, self-discipline and routine had started paying off. My grades improved, and life began to make more sense. I was learning some principles that would serve me well for the rest of my life. One of them was, "Simply obey first, and find out why later!" (I know many Christians who have not yet learned that lesson, and that is the first lesson in walking with God.)

It was amazing. I went from hating military life to missing it. There is a lot of freedom in discipline and routine. I did not even have to think about what to wear for two years. It was all predetermined for me! I sometimes wish I had made the military a career. It could have helped me, and it could help a lot of other inconsistent high *"I"* types.

That experience taught me a lot. Wherever you are, be all there. Learn what you need to know while you are in that specific set of circumstances. The present moment is happening for a reason.

As the saying goes, "The past is gone; the future is not here. All you have is today, and that is a gift. That is why it is called the present!" If you do not learn what you need to know now, you will have to learn it all over again in the future. So, get involved in the process of your own life and your current set of circumstances. If you cannot learn to be happy where you are, you will never be happy where you are not! Learn all you can. Let life teach you what you need to know.

Tip: Wherever you are, be all there!

36

Common sense will give you uncommon results!

Years ago when I was a school principal, I had to take a course in school law. The teacher gave us all of the current rules, regulations and procedures relating to the laws that govern the school environment. It was a very difficult class, and I remember taking a lot of notes!

It is funny that the one thing I remember above all else is that the teacher told us to use common sense. He gave us this example: If the maintenance man is mopping the lunchroom and somebody walks in, slips down and breaks his or her leg, you could find yourself in a lawsuit very easily. However, if you take the time to put a sign up that says, "Wet floor," you just acted in a "prudent manner." That will protect you from a lawsuit, and save your neck...and your wallet!

He said that in a court of law, a judge and a jury always look to see if you acted in a "prudent manner." In other words, did you take the time to use common sense?

Naturally, if someone walks through a room and does not know that the floor has been mopped, it would be very easy for that person to slip and fall down. However, if you put a sign up that warns people that the floor is wet, and they ignore or do not see the sign, that is not your fault. You tried your best to help people, even though they may not have tried to help themselves.

During that class, the teacher used the phrase "the prudent manner" over and over and over again. I came to the conclusion that acting in a "prudent manner" and using "common sense" are one and the same.

A good example of this happened to me last night. I was driving down the road, and it was raining. I saw a huge tractor-trailer truck that had pulled over to the side of the road. The driver had the hood of his cab raised, because evidently, he was having mechanical problems. What intrigued me about the situation was that he had put out huge, red, triangular markers behind his truck, along with turning on his hazardous blinking lights.

I thought to myself, "That driver just acted in a 'prudent manner.' He cannot help the fact that his truck broke down, and he cannot help the fact that he is on the side of the road off of an interstate highway. However, he can protect himself and others by having his warning lights flashing and by putting out huge markers on the road to warn people that they should be on extra alert!" In other words, he acted in a "prudent manner;" he used common sense.

Let me encourage you to stop looking at what someone else is doing right or wrong, and ask yourself if you are acting in a "prudent manner." The older I get, the more I see the value in thinking this way. Both you and I have encountered people that do not seem to think things though or use common sense. It can be frustrating! But rather than seeing what someone else is doing WRONG, why don't we see what we can do RIGHT to make things better in our own life and in the lives of others? In other words, this week act in a prudent manner! As a matter of fact, it will not hurt you to use this week's tip the rest of your life!

*Tip: Common sense
will give you uncommon results!*

37

Reevaluate where you are from time to time.

Have you ever noticed how easy it is to get stuck in a routine in life? Now, do not get me wrong. I believe routine can be a good thing. (My two years in military school taught me the value of living by routine and strict self-discipline.) What I am talking about is an altogether different matter.

As you can imagine, in my travels, I meet many people. I have been surprised by the vast majority of individuals that I have met who are dissatisfied with their life, but they seemingly do not know what to do about it. They have failed to learn how to discern the signals life is sending them. But, be encouraged, this tip will give you further help in that area!

Sometimes, we need to move out and go. Sometimes, we need to bring things to an end and stop. Other times, we need to simply sit still and wait, and that is where the difficulty lies. Because all of us have work to do, it is sometimes hard to discern when to hold on and when to let go. Our attitude and trust factor always play a huge part in the decision-making process.

We sometimes live in fear and think, "What will happen to me if my work dries up?" Well, here is the answer to that question: The same God that provided the last work you did is fully capable of providing you with more work to do! The secret is to discern or re-evaluate where you are in life and what keeps hindering your personal growth.

Years ago, someone taught me a valuable truth about life. The journey from where I currently am today to where I will be in a few years from now will NOT be like a plane ride from point A to point B. It will be more like a sailboat ride in a zigzag fashion. (That is called tacking against the wind. That is the way a sailboat ride occurs. It is perfectly normal and should be expected.) When I come to the end of a situation, I need to evaluate what I learned and how it can help me in the future.

I have come to see that when I think I am at the end of the road that I am currently traveling, in reality, I am simply at the beginning of a new road and a new start! God never quits working with us... never! He created us for a purpose and that purpose is not to simply frustrate us, but to teach us, guide us, help us and strengthen us. It is not an easy process, but anything in life that is valuable comes at a great price.

I once read that learning when to move and when

to stand still would be the greatest challenge any business-person would ever face. I have come to see that advice is true. Actually, this is very similar to the sailboat trip illustration. When the wind dies down, it may simply be time to reset the sails and turn in a new direction. And sometimes that requires us to be confused and live in darkness for a while. (The old puritans called this the dark night of the soul.)

The reason that we have darkness each day is to allow our eyes time to rest. Think about it. If we had light in our eyes all the time, it would wear our eyes out. Darkness is a gift to allow us down time to wait... and rest. Darkness does not last forever. God created the darkness as well as the light.

All of these simple illustrations help me put a "hook" on what is taking place around me each day. I do not want my life to simply be a bunch of random events without any meaning. I want to participate in the process of life. I want to learn what I need to learn. I want to experience this adventure. Don't you?

Tip: Reevaluate
where you are from time to time.

38

There is a huge difference between "privacy" and "secrecy."

Everyone has said, "I just need some time to be alone and be by myself." Everyone needs to be alone and experience "down time," even if it is simply to recover from exhaustion or an illness. That is known as privacy. There is nothing wrong with privacy. We all want it and expect it. After all, when you are using the restroom, privacy is a nice experience.

Secrecy, however, is another matter. When we want secrecy, it is usually because we are doing something that we should not be doing. We are trying to cover up our tracks and hide what we are doing. (I know. I have done it... and you have too!) If other people find out what we are doing, we will be embarrassed, or we will be in a lot of trouble.

There have been many books written about the personal damage that secrets can cause. (An example is *Family Secrets: What You Don't Know Can Hurt You* by John

Bradshaw.) The things we do in "darkness" are our secrets. When they are exposed to the "light," we see them for what they really are.

A lot has been said in recent days about the privacy laws in the U.S. because of the terrorist attacks. Everyone is screaming that we need to protect our privacy, and I am all for privacy. I am just not for secrecy. If people are living among us in secrecy, we need to expose them as soon as possible... and whatever it is that they are doing.

Think about this for a moment: If I try to use a credit card that has exceeded its limit or the bill has not been paid or if it has been reported lost or stolen, the bank behind that credit card stops its availability immediately. Why? Because they know that something is wrong and needs to be corrected before the credit card is available to be used. You are free to use the credit card in any way you wish (privacy) until you violate your agreement with them (secrecy). At that point, they want to talk to you in order to resolve the situation.

I am all for privacy. But when you are deliberately trying to hide something, you have moved to secrecy. Do you know what follows secrecy? After secrecy comes deception, lies, pain, broken relationships, heartache, humiliation, tears, loneliness, sorrow and sadness. Ask Jim Bakker, Jimmy Swaggart, Richard Nixon, the Keating Five, Ivan Bolsky and Michael Milken. It is a downward spiral. One from which it is difficult to recover.

Is there anything that you are trying to hide? What

is the one secret that you do not want exposed to the light? What is that one deep, dark secret that grips your heart in fear every time you think about it being made public for all to know?

Let me encourage you to refuse to have secrets. In time, they will destroy you. Find an accountability partner with whom you can share your secrets. In that manner, you will "break" the power of the secret, and then it will lose its power to destroy your life.

Privacy is a good thing. If you have nothing to hide, why should you be afraid? Secrecy is a bad thing. It hurts you as well as others.

My daughter, Esther, says that secrecy is "shady-cat" living. That pretty much sums it up!

Tip: There is a huge difference between "privacy" and "secrecy."

39

Begin using your R.A.S.
(Reticular Activating System).

I can just hear a lot of you right now saying, "Use my what? My R.A.S? I did not know that I had one!"

Well, neither did I! I did not know anything about it at one time in my life. Now it has become one of my best resources of information! This week, I want you to get better acquainted with your R.A.S.

The Reticular Activating System is a built-in device designed by our Creator to help you better succeed at finding things in which you are interested. You have a network of cells that function every day to help you receive (or allow in) valuable information into your mind. When you are looking for specific information, your R.A.S. starts searching for it.

Have you ever misplaced your keys? When you start looking for them, have you ever noticed what happens? Your eyes start getting focused on looking for keys. Your hands start helping by moving stuff around to see where the keys could possibly be. Your brain starts thinking, "Where was the last place I used my keys? What did I do next? Where did I go, and then what did I do?" In other words, everything starts working together to help you find your keys!

The Reticular Activating System also acts as a filter to keep out harmful or unwanted information. Have you ever been at a movie and all of a sudden a "gory" scene appeared on the screen? If you closed your eyes or turned your head to look away, you just received help from your R.A.S.

Again, this network of cells function all the time to help you receive in helpful information or filter out unwanted information.

Tip: Begin using your R.A.S.
(Reticular Activating System).

40

Be Grateful!

Every year around Thanksgiving time, I feel extremely grateful for a lot of things: my health, my family, my friends, my business and co-workers, my church, my men's fellowship accountability group, my relationships and my country. Since I have had the opportunity to travel all over the world, I can tell you from firsthand experience, that there is no place as wonderful as the U.S.A. (At least, that is my opinion!)

Do you have a grateful heart? Are you aware of the truth that the 8 most important facts about your life were all totally out of your control? That's right! The 8 most important issues that have influenced everything about your life and who you are were all completely out of your control. You had nothing to do with any of them; yet, they have shaped your life to help make you the person that you are today. Let's take a look at each one of them.

1. WHERE YOU WERE BORN - You could have been born anywhere on the planet or even not at all! You could have been born in a big city or a small town; a free country or a communist country; a country full of opportunities and resources or a country on the brink of starvation with little hope for advancement.

2. THE TIME IN HISTORY IN WHICH YOU WERE BORN - You could have been born several thousand years ago or several hundred years from now. You could have lived during the time when the world was thought to be flat. You could have been born at a time in which there was little known information in science or medicine or aviation or communications. You could have been born during a time of war or peace. You could have been born during a time when there was good technology or no technology at all!

3. WHO YOUR PARENTS WERE - Your mother and father helped create you before you even met them! They determined your race, your genes and your unique DNA pattern and to some degree your intelligence. Their physical bodies were the tools used to get you here in the first place. And just think... they never even asked you if you wanted to be born! (But, I am betting that you are glad that they got you here!)

4. YOUR EARLY CHILDHOOD EDUCATION - You really had little say or interest in your education until

you were in high school or college. Most psychologists agree that your early formative years are some of the most important years of your life. Being exposed to information, music, different languages, different family members, kindergarten and elementary school teachers, reading, writing, arithmetic, friends, neighbors - all contributed to how you view the world. All of that shaped your view of the world as a friendly place or a hostile place.

5. YOUR HEALTH - You were nurtured and fed by others for years. What they fed you helped create your health. If you were fed a balanced diet, your body responded by giving you good health and a nice figure. But sadly, if you ate fat, greasy food, well, you may have ended up a fat, greasy dude! (I don't say that to be unkind. It just is a fact of life that what we eat, for the most part, creates our outer appearance.) This is why it is especially important for parents to oversee what their children eat and give their children a balanced diet whether they like it or not! (I am still grateful my mother gave me vegetables rather than french fries, and, by the way, she never gave me a choice! I never even knew one was available!)

6. YOUR SIBLINGS - You had nothing to do with your birth order nor how many brother or sisters you have. Your parents pretty much decided that issue for you. Some pregnancies are planned. Some are surprises. The

point is that you are now here and who your brothers and sisters are was always totally out of your control. I heard Zig Ziglar say that he was tenth born out of twelve children. Zig once asked his mother, "Why did you have so many children?"

She replied, "Well, after which child do you think we should have stopped?"

Well, it certainly was not before him! And that is the whole point. If you have brothers or sisters, cherish them. They are the siblings that you were destined to have!

7. YOUR SOCIO-ECONOMIC STATUS - Some of you were born into wealthy families, while others of you were born in poverty... or somewhere in-between. Your environment and the worldly possessions that you had while growing up were a direct result of your parents' financial position. I have seen wealth hurt some people, and I have seen poverty help some people. In either case, while you were growing up, you probably were not very aware of what you had or what you did not have. If your family was well-off financially, you may have been able to do a little more or have more opportunities. (In either case, your family's finances had little to do with the fact that they loved you and wanted you to have a good life.)

8. GOD'S LOVE FOR YOU - You did nothing to cause

God to love you. He wanted to do that. He has always loved you. You did nothing spectacular to get his attention. And, your worse sins have not stopped him from loving you. As long as you are alive, he will continue to love you. He has a good plan for your life.

There you have it… the 8 most important facts about your life. They are the things that have helped shape who you are, and they were all out of your control. You cannot do anything about them either, except perhaps grow in your education, improve your health and better your financial future.

I suggest that you realize the power of gratitude. Learn to see the results of things that happened before you got here and realize that they were all part of the plan for you. If you are grateful, reflect back on why you are grateful, and let someone who was in your "8 - step circle of influence" know about it. It will mean a lot to him or her.

Tip: Be Grateful!

41

There is a big difference between a "peacekeeper" and a "peacemaker."

The older I get, the more I notice and understand the finer distinctions in life. It is easy to go through life looking on the surface of everything. Unfortunately, it is also more painful. In order to be truly successful, a person must learn to look beneath the surface and see the underlying issues. This brings awareness to what is actually happening. The following example will bring greater clarity to this idea.

Growing up, I was taught to be a peacekeeper. To me, that meant that I needed to do everything in my power to get along with everyone else. It also meant that I should try to help other people get along with each other. (The concept is similar to being a mediator.) I remember thinking, "If I can just get Daddy to be nicer to Mama, we will all be a lot happier." Did you ever think that way as a child regarding your parents or siblings?

You might think, "What is wrong with that idea?" I can tell you - plenty! If your goal is to go through life with that kind of mind-set, in time, it will cause you to develop an unhealthy, co-dependency mentality. Your own happiness and stability will begin to be based on how well everyone around you is getting along with each other.

I believe former President Jimmy Carter had a peace-keeper mentality. He worked hard on a Middle East peace agreement. He actually thought he could meet with the leaders of two countries (Israel and Egypt), whose people had not gotten along for several thousand years, and talk them into signing a piece of paper, go home and everything would begin to be different for their respective people. Needless to say, time has demonstrated that methodology to be futile.

President Carter used a similar tactic, when U.S. citizens were taken hostage in Iran. Carter tried to negotiate with the Iranian government, using the embargo strategy. He was dedicated to continuing the process of talking to people in order to keep an open dialogue going. He thought that would ensure a peaceful settlement. After 444 days, it proved to be an unsuccessful way to handle the situation. Both of these foreign policy examples demonstrate the mentality of a peacekeeper.

On the other hand, there is the mentality of the peace-maker. This view says, "Do what is right. Take all the available information known at the time, consult with your very best people and then make a firm decision regardless of who it upsets or what the outcome may be."

I believe that Ronald Reagan had that kind of mentality. He publicly declared, "Mr. Gorbachev, open this gate!

Mr. Gorbachev, tear down this wall!" (He was referring to the Berlin Wall that separated East Berlin and communism from West Berlin and freedom.) Reagan was also the one who said, "My first act after I am sworn in as President will be to go get our hostages in Iran with a strong and powerful hand." However, Reagan didn't have to forcefully take action with Iran. The day he was sworn in as the new President, the hostages were all released. You see, that is what a peacemaker does. He or she does what is right at all cost and pretty soon other people catch on and fall in line.

I believe that our current President, George W. Bush, is a peacemaker. The next time you are in Iraq, ask the majority of the Iraqi people what they think, as well as the new President of Iraq what he thinks!

And since I am on a roll. . . I believe that the first President Bush (George H. W.) began his presidency as a peacemaker, "I will tell congress to read my lips - no new taxes," but ended up a peacekeeper, "I am working with the congress on a new tax package. . ." Also note, that the senior Bush attacked Iraq with decisiveness, and then let Sadaam stay in power, because he thought he was no longer a threat! Did that help get him reelected? How did the American people handle a peacekeeper like the senior George Bush? They handled him the same way that they handled Jimmy Carter. They sent him home without reelecting him to a second term. There is something deep inside every one of us that wants a peacemaker to be our leader.

I now see that when I was growing up, it would have

Robert A. Rohm Ph.D.

been a lot healthier for me, although a lot harder, to simply tell my father, "It does not seem to me that you hold your wife and my mother in very high regard. I would appreciate it if you would set a better example for me and help me learn how to be a better man in that area."

I know, I know, you think I am nuts. And, that is okay with me. I have learned the power and secret of healthy thinking. It is found in being a peacemaker not a peacekeeper!

Just last week, I invited a friend to go to church with me. He told me that he might come. I gently, but specifically said, "I would prefer a *no* or *yes*. I will accept either one. I simply need a commitment one way or the other in order to make my plans." He then told me *no*, which I lovingly and kindly accepted. The funny thing is that on Sunday, he showed up at church! I have learned that someone who says, "I might be there," just gave you the code word to create craziness in your life... the word "might." You will always be living with unfilled expectations.

At one time in my life, I did not know what to do with those kind of responses from other people. But that was when I wanted to be a peacekeeper. Now I know how to simply ask for a commitment one way or the other, fully offering, "Either way is okay." I have seen a lot more success with that finer distinction. But, after all, now I understand the difference between being a peacekeeper and being a peacemaker. One way creates confusion while the other way creates direction.

The older I get, the wiser I want to become. Think

142

about this tip. I am not asking you to agree with me, because you might not want to. But, that is okay. You have been wrong before, and you will be wrong again. So, will I. I am simply focusing in on a finer distinction... one that will make you healthy (mentally), wealthy (financially) and wise (relationally).

Blessed are the peacemakers!

Tip: There is a big difference between a "peacekeeper" and a "peacemaker."

42

There is a huge difference between being "remorseful" and being "repentant."

All of us have made mistakes in our life. That is part of the human condition. Sometimes when we realize we have done something wrong (either towards ourselves or towards another person), we apologize for our actions. There is nothing wrong with apologizing to another person or even to ourselves for that matter. However, over the years, I have discovered a real secret to learning from my mistakes which helps me to do better the next time around. That secret has to do with having a repentant attitude, not simply having a remorseful attitude.

People who are remorseful will apologize for what they have done. They will usually say they are sorry and oftentimes show deep humility. However, all of us have probably had people tell us that they are sorry, but in a short time, they turn right back around and do the same thing again to us or to another person. That is because they were remorseful rather than repentant.

People who are truly repentant realize that what they

did was wrong, and they have a strong desire to change their behavior. They recognize that they have been heading in the wrong direction, and they want to go in a different direction. Although they are remorseful, it goes much deeper than that. They come to see the deep hurt they have caused themselves and others as well as God. Their heartfelt attitude becomes one of taking specific steps to not repeat the same behaviors over and over again.

Perhaps you have heard of King Saul, the first king of Israel. He deliberately went against the commands of God. Both he and the army of Israel suffered greatly for it. When Saul was confronted with his behavior, he was very remorseful, but not repentant. You might say he was sorry that he got caught.

Then you have the second king of Israel, King David. When he was confronted with his disobedience to God, the first words out of his mouth were, "I have sinned against the Lord." That is an attitude of repentance. Saul was sorry that he got caught. David was sorry that he offended God.

This tip is not meant to sound like a bedtime Bible story. Rather, it is meant to teach a very deep lesson; namely, you can grow better and faster when you are willing to admit your mistakes, face your issues and walk in a new direction.

Which of the following two sentences would you rather hear when someone is apologizing to you?

1. I'm sorry.
2. I was wrong; please forgive me.

I think you get the idea. This week, let me encourage you to begin to open your eyes to the possibility of the part that you have played in hurting another person. You may have apologized to that person, but the behavior still may be present inside of you. It would be far better to correct the actions than to simply keep apologizing. I once heard a pastor say, "God isn't much into apologies, but he loves repentance." I believe that is true.

Tip: There is a huge difference between being "remorseful" and being "repentant."

43

Be productive
without being abusive.

One of the more celebrated television shows at this time is "The Apprentice." I have only watched one episode, so I do not know everything that is involved with the show. The big idea, however, is for several outstanding young men and women to compete against one another to see who can do the best job for Donald Trump. I believe the winner is going to actually get to work on his staff for a year.

The interesting dynamic that has caught my attention in this "reality" show is the fact that each week someone gets fired. There seems to be a twinkle in Donald Trump's eyes when he fires one of the contestants. The commercials that are used to promote the show always include a clip of Trump saying, "You're fired!"

Recently, a friend of mine and I were talking about the fact that these reality T.V. shows are actually non-reality! You cannot build a business, a family, a church or a country by getting rid of people. You can only learn to build a great organization by growing people and developing their potential. If someone does not measure up to the expectation of his or her employer, or mom or dad, etc., that person can be coached or worked with until he or she learns how to do the job better. I realize that not everyone will achieve high levels of success instantly in life. We are all competent in different ways. Even when someone does make a mistake, there is no real reason to be abusive to him or her. It is much better to point out what could have been done better by attacking the problem rather than firing someone and attacking the person.

I am not trying to attack this T.V. program. I have just lived long enough to know that when people make a mistake, they are far more likely to grow through the process if someone encourages them and works with them rather than attacks them.

All of the jobs I have had in the past in which someone was abusive with me taught me very little. However, all of the jobs I have had in the past where someone helped me to learn and grow when I made a mistake has helped me to be a better person.

This week, learn to look for ways to be more productive with people all around you, especially your children. It is easy to "fuss" at others when they do not do what you want them to do. It may make you feel better, but it does them very little good. By being helpful and kind and not abusive, you will see everyone around you become more productive. That is a reality show you can count on!

Tip: Be productive without being abusive.

44

When you admit that you are blind, you will be able to see!

One of the hardest things to do is to point out to another person his or her faults. You don't want to do it, and that person doesn't want to hear it! Unless a person is very mature as well as secure in his or her personhood, chances are that your words of guidance, reproof and correction will fall on deaf ears. As the old saying goes, "He who is convinced against his will is of the same opinion still!"

Recently, in a training program that I was conducting, I reviewed the blind spots of each of the four personality types. This information is not given in order to hurt anyone's feelings. It is given in order to help everyone to be able to see some things that perhaps he or she failed to see earlier in life:

"*D*"- Don't push; give others time to process and think; use softer tones.

"*I*"- Be organized; stick to the goal; stay focused.

"*S*"- Remember that challenges are good; give realistic commitments; remember that F.E.A.R. is only False Evidence Appearing Real.

"*C*"- Don't get caught up in too much detail; keep in mind the person versus the process; remember to smile and be cordial.

As I reflected upon each one of these, I remembered the time that I met with a new friend who is a high "*I*" type. He knew nothing about personality styles. We met in a restaurant to discuss some of the challenges that he was facing in his life.

After we had been there for about an hour, I asked him a question, "Do you find it odd that we have been together for an hour and you have talked 59 minutes and I have talked 1? Does that seem balanced to you?"

He just sat there and stared at me. He was processing what I had just said to him. Again, I did not say this to hurt his feelings nor did I say it to try to look good or be superior to him in any way. The only reason that I pointed it out was to try to help him wake up to one of the reasons that he was in the mess he was in at that time in his life. He was a great talker but a poor listener. (I know that club! I have been the past president!) At any rate, after a while, he seemed to be able to receive what I was trying to say to him.

Again, when you talk to another person, remember to use correct voice tones and always speak gently - remembering that you have some blind spots and weaknesses of your own! I also add that it is always a good idea to have this kind of conversation alone in a place where an individual feels safe, rather than embarrassing that person in front of his or her friends.

Now, I realize that a blind spot is not called a blind spot because you can see it. It is called a blind spot, because you are blind to it! Therefore, the question naturally arises, "How can I see something I do not see?" Another way to state this idea is, "How can I possibly open my eyes to an area to which I am blind?"

I have discovered that there are a few things you can do:

1. Ask yourself what areas cause you to continuously stumble. For example, years ago, I thought I had a pretty good grasp of understanding money. After reading several of Robert Kiyosaki's books, my eyes began to slowly open. I discovered I had actually known very little about money! In other words, I discovered that although I thought I could see, I was actually blind in that area.
2. Ask a close friend if he or she sees some areas of your life that could use some improvement. Notice that I used the words "close friend." If the person does not know you well, he or she will not be able to help you very much.
3. Ask God to begin to help you see new truths in the areas that have previously tripped you up. Ask him to

help you walk in these new truths. No one wants to help you more in your weak areas than God! He even says in 2 Corinthians 12:9 NIV, "My grace is sufficient for you, for my power is made perfect in weakness."

Some tips are exciting to practice, while others are more difficult to face. This one is a little more difficult. But, it pays rich rewards to all those who are willing to have their eyes opened regardless of how painful it is.

Tip: When you admit that you are blind, you will be able to see!

45

Never again say, "I forgot."

Many years ago, I was a school teacher, and I later became a school principal. The one statement that I heard over and over again from my students that drove me crazy was, "I forgot." I heard it several times every day. I often wondered if there was a contagious disease going around the school called, "IFORGOTITUS!"

One day, I was having a conversation with a middle school young lady. After she told me that she had forgotten something, I looked at her and said, "What does that mean?"

She looked back at me like I was crazy. She said, "You know, I forgot!"

I looked at her and said, "No, I don't know. What does that mean?"

Again, she said, "I just forgot."

I decided to press the issue. I asked, "What plan did you put into place in order to help you remember?"

She asked, "What do you mean?"

I said, "Well, did you write yourself a note, or did you create a way to help yourself succeed?"

She said, "No, I just thought I would remember."

I asked, "Did your plan work?"

She said, "No."

I was surprised at what came out of my mouth next. I said to her, "Please do not ever again say to me, 'I forgot' as long as you live. I cannot and will not accept those two words. I will accept it if you say, 'I failed to plan to succeed,' but I cannot accept, 'I forgot' any longer."

I spent a few minutes explaining to her that "I forgot" was a totally irresponsible way for anyone to live his or her life. No one on the earth can remember everything. The secret to remembering things is to have a plan to succeed. It usually means creating a system to write yourself a note to help yourself succeed in remembering what you have to do.

Before she left my office, she promised me that she would never again say, "I forgot."

In a couple of weeks, I saw her in the hall. I stopped her and asked her about something that she had promised me she would do. She looked at me and said, "I failed to plan to succeed, but I will go write it down and have it for you tomorrow!" The next day, she kept her promise. She later told me that "planning to succeed" was a lot better than saying "I forgot."

What about you? Do you often catch yourself

saying, "I forgot"? I am not trying to make a mountain out of a molehill. I am simply trying to promote personal responsibility, good mental health and individual success. It will never happen if you think, "I forgot" is acceptable.

Start saying, "I failed to plan to succeed," the next time you forget something and watch what you start doing differently in the future. I promise that if you practice this tip, you will soon drop two words out of your vocabulary... "I forgot!"

Tip: Never again say, "I forgot."

46

People fail because of broken focus.

ecently, I have become more and more aware of how easy it is to get sidetracked in life. Have you ever noticed how many different things pull you in different directions? Some examples are bills, pets, phone calls, laundry, relatives, yard work, health challenges, gasoline fill–ups, paperwork, friends, weather considerations, luncheon appointments, straightening out miscommunications, birthdays, political matters that need your input, unexpected interruptions and the list goes on and on and on! All of these things are important, and none of them can be ignored forever. (If you do not pay attention to small matters, it will not be long before they become things that really matter!) I am not suggesting that you ignore these things. Instead, I am saying that you should not allow them to divert your attention away from your primary focus, your mission, your goal, your life!

After the death of Moses, when Joshua was leading

the Israelites into the promised land, God spoke directly to him. (You can read the entire encounter in Joshua chapter one.) As I was recently rereading the story, there was one comment that caught my eye, "Be careful to obey all the laws my servant Moses gave you; do not turn from it to the right or to the left, that you may be successful wherever you go."*

As I reflected upon the command that the Lord gave to Joshua, I asked myself a question, "Why would God take the time to tell Joshua not to turn to the right or to the left?" Then I read the rest of the sentence, and I saw my answer, "That you may be successful wherever you go."

If there is one thing my own experience has taught me, it is this: I cannot be halfway committed to something and expect to get wholehearted results. If I do not pay attention to the things that I know I have been called to do, it will not be long before other things begin to get me off track. If I am working on something and give it my full attention, then over time, I can count on one thing to happen, namely, success.

About 100 years ago, there were three enterprises under way that would forever change the course of human history. In 1903, Ford Motor Company, Harley-Davidson Motor Company and the first flight by the Wright brothers in Kitty Hawk, North Carolina. Isn't that interesting? These three ideas were all being developed by three different groups of people, in three different parts of the country who, as far as I know, had no daily interaction with one another. They were all hard at work. Each had very different ideas. Yet, they all had one strong common trait: focus! And what has been the result? Success!

Do you see what I mean? When we get sidetracked and bogged down, our focus gets broken and in turn, we lose our success. In other words, it is not the interruptions in my life that cause me to fail. All of us have interruptions. It is the broken focus that becomes deadly. I cannot afford to lose my focus.

This week let me encourage you to keep your primary focus in mind. Then, success will be guaranteed!

Tip: People fail because of broken focus.

* Joshua 1:7b NIV

47

Remember that the decision-making process should be the fourth step in the change process; otherwise you will make poor, weak decisions.

Have you ever wondered why some people seemingly make good decisions, and others do not? Well, I have news for you. It is not luck or fate or random happenstance that causes all that to occur. There are time-tested, proven steps that you can learn to use to be a better decision maker and thus become more successful in all that you do. Let us review them together:

1. Awareness – you cannot beware of something that you are not first aware of. Awareness is when you begin to see things in a different way or in a new light. Your lens or filter or paradigm takes a shift, and you start to notice things that you have overlooked or ignored in the past.

2. Understanding – you start asking questions or reading more information on your newfound interest. You suddenly find a lot of good information that had pre-

viously been unknown to you. You meet new people who give you information that has taken them years and years to acquire. You feel that you have suddenly awakened to life.

3. Belief / Acceptance / Buy-in – this is when you start to "own" this new information. You embrace it and make it part of your life. No one has to talk you into anything any longer. You have become a "believer" for yourself. You start talking to other people in a more convincing manner. You are no longer simply a student. You have become a teacher as well.

4. Decision / Commitment – this is the crucial step. It is here that you make a firm decision or commitment that something is about to change. Because of what has transpired in steps 1, 2 and 3, your roots go deep. You become firmly entrenched in your new way of thinking. You "get it," you "see it" and you want to "do it!"

5. Action (with modification) – at this step, you are no longer concerned with whether or not you are making a right decision. Your thinking has changed. The key now is to make the wisest decision possible, and then make it right! In other words, get going! If things need slight adjustments, then modify them as you go. If you get lost or confused, then ask for directions along the way. Stop thinking that everyone knows what he or she is doing. Truly successful people are simply failures who kept on going!

6. Know the reasons / causes for success or failure – now you can look back at what you just experienced and see how you got the results that occurred (regardless of what happened – in a relationship, a career change – a new purchase – or a business decision). If things went well, you will want to repeat the same steps of action in the future. If things went poorly, you will now know where you need to make some major improvements next time. You are free from insanity - you no longer do the same thing and expect to get different results!

By using these six simple steps, you will begin to see that there are specific steps to help you in building your personal life, your family life or your financial future. The more you know about what you are doing and why you are doing it, the more successful you will become.

I have learned to ask myself which step I am on in the decision-making process. When I know, I stay focused on that step until I am ready to move to the next one. It has made me wiser, more emotionally stable and better off in financial matters. It will work for you, too! Try it this week. Practice these six steps, and you will soon see better results from your improved decision-making ability.

Tip: Remember that the decision-making process should be the fourth step in the change process; otherwise you will make poor, weak decisions.

48

Feed all 3 parts of yourself daily.

Most of us eat food every day. It comes naturally to you and me. Very few of us have ever needed an eating lesson. We are all natural-born eaters! But, have you ever stopped and thought about the fact that there are actually three parts to ourselves that we need to feed daily?

The first part is our body. Let's start there, because that is the area in which all of us already excel. You and I usually eat two or three times every day. Many of the new diets actually encourage you to eat five or six times daily in order to lose weight. I don't think I need to belabor the point concerning feeding our bodies. Everyone knows that has to happen in order to live. But there are three areas that we need to nurture, and unfortunately, this one is the only area that many people choose to focus on and feed.

The second area is our soul. That part of us includes our mind, will and emotions. We can feed this part of ourselves by reading good, positive, mental attitude books or listening to similar-type audiotapes. For example, most average drivers spend several hundred hours each year in their car driving from one location to another during the day. Why not turn driving time into learning time? You could become one of the best-educated people in your field, simply by listening to audio programs rather than always choosing music.

There are many factors that affect the health of our soul. We often overlook the fact that our friends, the movies we watch, the music we hear and the places we go, all have an impact on our soul, whether we realize it or not. Our daily choices influence our attitudes, and I believe a positive attitude is one of the most important qualities any person could possess. I like what Zig Ziglar says, "A positive attitude won't MAKE you do anything, but it will HELP you do EVERYTHING better."

Our souls need to be nurtured daily. Our thoughts, words, actions, attitudes and deeds proceed from our mind, will and emotions. The way we think, the words we say, the desire to keep trying harder or to keep working smarter, all come from our soul. The emotions of excitement, happiness, joy, sorrow, sadness, loneliness and the other feelings that we experience, are all part of life. However, to not be controlled or dominated by emotions is another story. We can only keep our emotions from dominating our life if our soul is well fed and healthy. Our soul's health stems from the way we think. As Proverbs 23:7a KJV tells us, "For as he (a person) thinketh in his heart, so is he."

The third area is our spirit. This is the part of us that will live forever. Actually, this is the real you. Long after your body is gone, your spirit will still be alive. You were created to live forever! That amazes me. Billions and billions and billions of years from now, you will still be alive.

The spirit part of you is that part of you that was "created in God's image." Think about it for just a second. What does it mean to be "created in the image of God?" Well, it isn't talking about your body. You are not that good looking! It isn't talking about your soul. You are not that smart! It is talking about your spirit. You were designed to live forever. As you grow in the knowledge of spiritual things, you will get so happy that you will run problems and challenges right out of your life, because you will learn to see things from an eternal perspective.

Decide today to recognize God's power at work in your life. Feed your spirit daily with truths from the Bible or other good devotional literature. Man should not live by bread alone, but by the wisdom and truth that comes from the Father above.

This week, start the daily habit of feeding all three parts of yourself. You will see an immediate improvement. You will see all three areas start to turn you into the person that you desire to be!

Tip: Feed all 3 parts of yourself daily.

49

Understand how
people build relationships.

his tip is based on the DISC Model of Human Behavior. It is also known as the D-I-S-C circle. To review: the top half of the circle represents people who are more outgoing. The bottom half represents people who are more reserved. The left side of the circle represents people who are more task-oriented. The right side represents people who are more people-oriented. Then, you add the four letters D-I-S-C in clockwise order starting in the upper left-hand quadrant, and you can see the Model of Human Behavior. (See the graphics in the "Before You Start" section.) This gives you the four basic personality types: the "*D*" (Dominant type), the "*I*" (Inspiring type), the "*S*" (Supportive type) and the "*C*" (Cautious type).

Each of the four personality types builds relationships in a different manner. The "*D*" and the "*C*" types are both more task-oriented. Therefore, almost everything they do is viewed through the lens or filter of a task. To them, relationships need to include a goal or purpose. However, the "*I*" and the "*S*" types are more people-oriented. Therefore, almost everything they do is done with an emotional connection in mind. They simply do not want anyone to be left out. This does not mean that one side of the equation (in the Model of Human Behavior) is better than the other. They are simply different.

The point I want to make in this week's tip is the fact that because "*D*" and "*C*" types are more task- oriented, they tend to build relationships as a task. For example, if "*Ds*" or "*Cs*" want to build a relationship with you, it simply becomes another item they add to their "to do" list. If they happen to be connecting with another "*D*" or "*C*" type, then the task of building a relationship is a rather simple process. However, if they are trying to build a relationship with an "*I*" or "*S*" type, and they do it through the lens or filter of a task, it comes across as almost rude or abrupt. An "*I*" or an "*S*" type would tell you that instead of it feeling warm and friendly, it almost feels offensive! You were simply part of their "to do" list, and after they spoke to you and gave you a few minutes of their time, now they were relieved of that duty.

I realize these words might seem a little harsh to a "*D*" or "*C*" type. That is not my intention at all. The purpose of this tip is to help everyone, especially "*D*" and "*C*" types, to become wise in building relationships. (In the next tip, we will help the "*I*" and "*S*" types learn to do tasks better, because they tend to be weaker in that area.)

This week, let me encourage everyone who has a high

"*D*" type or "*C*" type personality to stay a little more focused on being warm and friendly as you try to connect with the "*I*" or "*S*" type individual. Do not make it a task when trying to connect with them, but actually make it a real endeavor to be relational, warm and friendly. Start your sentences with, "Hi, how are you feeling today. It is good to see you!" And remember to really mean it!

You will see a much better connection when you try this method. You will be glad that you learned to use it with all of your relationships both now and in the future.

Tip: Understand how people build relationships.

50

Understand how
people become task-oriented.

ast week our tip focused on learning to be more relational and people-oriented. This week we want to follow up to give more time to the "other side" in order to develop our task abilities as well.

Most of the *"D"* and *"C"* types are very task-oriented. They are efficient and effective in most everything they do. The main motivation for the *"D"* type is results. Some of the main motivations for the *"C"* type are quality answers, value and being right. (We always like to give extra details for the *"C"* type in order to get it just right!)

Because the *"I"* and *"S"* types are both more people-oriented, they have a difficult time staying focused on tasks. To this personality type, who is primarily people-oriented, any task almost becomes a burden. A task does not carry with it the same amount of enthusiasm as meeting a new friend or beginning an adventure.

Both the *"I"* and the *"S"* types are easily sidetracked.

They can have great intentions, but unfortunately, many of those intentions go unfulfilled. For example, the "*I*" type is a great starter, but a poor finisher. They lose interest after the project gets going. The "*S*" type is a poor starter, but a good finisher. They have a very difficult time being motivated enough to get a new project started in the first place. In both of those instances, the main issue is once again the task.

This is not to infer in any manner that the "*I*" or "*S*" type personality is lazy or uncaring when it comes to a task. Once again, a task just does not carry with it the excitement and enthusiasm that a relationship does for these two particular personality types.

I would suggest that the "*Is*" and "*Ss*" write down each day what they want to see accomplished. I believe it was J.C. Penny who had the suggestion of starting each day by making a list. Then, number the list. Next, complete the number one item on the list, and do not stop until it is finished. After number one is completed, then proceed to #2 and #3 and so on. At the end of the day, you will be able to see that you were able to accomplish the goals and projects you set out for yourself. I personally have found this to be a very good method for getting tasks done in my own life. To the "*D*" and "*C*" types accomplishing a task almost comes as second nature. All of us can learn to emulate their determination and focus in accomplishing tasks.

It is easy to see from this tip (as well as last week's tip) that each personality type brings a special trait to the relationship mix. Some bring the ability to get tasks done, while others bring the ability to be warm and friendly in the process. One is not right or wrong. One is not good or bad. They are just different.

This week, why not try to stay focused on being more successful by accomplishing the tasks that you want to see done in your life? You will feel better as you watch your life make progress!

*Tip: Understand how
people become task-oriented.*

Be discreet when making a request.

When my children were growing up, they often had requests like all children do. They wanted a friend to be able to come over for dinner with our family or to go roller skating with us on Saturday afternoon or to be able to spend the night at our home on Friday night.

There is nothing wrong with any of those requests. However, I soon discovered that a problem could arise very quickly when they would ask me in an indiscreet manner. For example, if my daughter Esther wanted her friend Mary to spend the night at our house, Esther would ask me if that was all right while Mary stood right next to her. Well, that made me feel very uncomfortable. If the answer was *yes*, then there was no problem. However, occasionally if the answer had to be *no* (because of some set of circumstances), then I felt badly, Esther felt embarrassed and poor Mary felt hurt and rejected!

If you are a parent, you have discovered that

parenting comes with very little instruction. Much of what we know has been learned by "on the job training." Life can be a very good teacher if we choose to learn the lessons it is trying to teach us. However, the lessons often come painfully slow, and it takes time to "catch on" as to how to best use the information we are learning.

I sat Esther down, and we had a talk. I told her that I liked her friend Mary a lot, but I did not want to be put on the spot like that ever again. So that day in the Rohm household, we came up with a new policy: If you ask about anything that includes one of your friends and the friend is standing there and can hear your request, then the answer will automatically be *no*. Even if the answer would have been *yes*, it will automatically become *no*, because you failed to be discreet when making your request.

Well, you talk about an about face! I never saw anything work so well in all my life. Here was wisdom that would make Solomon proud! I believe God gave me that solution. I am not that smart!

I can honestly say that I do not believe that we ever had a problem with that issue again. Esther told me, "You know something Dad, even if I think the answer might be *no*, I at least have a 50-50 chance that it might be *yes*, if I ask correctly. But, I know if I put you on the spot it will be a *no* for sure!"

My children made their share of mistakes growing up. So did I. So did you! However, I am grateful that they learned some manners regarding the feelings of other people. I believe this was largely a result of learning discretion about what to say, and when to say it.

This week, take a closer look at how you may unknowingly put other people on the spot. Be discreet about what you say and in front of whom you say it. Realize that some requests can potentially be embarrassing or inappropriate. If you have children, why not begin to incorporate the principle mentioned in this tip. Help them see the possible damage that can be done to themselves and others when they do not take into account possible circumstances beyond your control. Teach them to use wisdom and discretion, and at least they will have better odds of seeing their requests, ideas and dreams come true!

Tip: Be discreet when making a request.

"... but not you!"

Perhaps many of you have heard of the famous motivational speaker by the name of Jim Rohn. I cannot tell you how many times someone has gotten Jim and me mixed up. It has not been because of our looks or even because of the message we teach. It is primarily because of our last names. His is R-o-h-n, and mine is R-o-h-m. There is only a one letter difference in our last names. So, I can see how some people can get the two of us mixed up from time to time.

As I mentioned earlier, Jim is a positive, motivational speaker. His writings and teachings have had a great influence on my life, as well as the lives of many other people. One of his famous thoughts is the following:

"Let others lead small lives, but not you.
Let others argue over small things, but not you.
Let others cry over small hurts, but not you.
Let others leave their future in someone else's hand, but not you!" *

As I recently reflected on that thought, I was once again reminded that if you want to be different in your daily life, then you are going to have to behave in a manner that is different from the rest of the pack! I am sure you have heard the old saying, "Cream always rises to the top." That is simply another way of saying what Jim has already said. All of us need to rise above the small things in life that are always trying to pull us down.

If you think back to your teenage years, you will remember how easy it was to have a "herd" mentality. I am fascinated by teenagers to this very day. Teenagers do not want anybody to tell them what to do. Yet, almost all of them lead a life of simply following the crowd. If one person that is popular, wears his or her baseball cap backwards, then all the teens begin to wear their baseball cap backwards. Isn't it ironic? They have an attitude that says, "I don't want anyone telling me what to do!" Nevertheless, it sure seems like everyone is telling them what to do!

That is part of growing up and part of the teenage process. We all went through it, and fortunately, most of us have grown out of it. Our children will as well.

The point I would like to make in this week's tip is that you are special, and you must rise above the small things in life that will tend to pull you down and sink your ship. I imagine that there has only been one or two major catastrophes to take place in your entire life. Yet there has probably been hundreds of small things that wear you out and pull you down every day.

This week, why not focus on the simple thought of rising above all that? If other people want to lead small lives and be disgruntled and upset about every single thing, then that is up to them. But, that is not for you! If other people want to argue over small things, let them argue. You will find that if you walk away, you will really be the bigger person. Let other people cry over the small hurts that are in their life. When you stop to realize how good you really do have it, you realize many of your small hurts really could be overlooked, because they are actually insignificant. When other people want to leave their future in the hands of unknown fate, you can choose to do all you reasonably can to make wise choices that will produce good results in your own life.

If you are normal, this practice will not be easy. It is always easier to slide toward mediocrity rather than excellence. But, with just a little thought and effort, we can all grow and rise above the pettiness in life and become effective in all we do.

Tip: "… but not you!"

---

* Jim Rohn (www.jimrohn.com) quote used by permission.

About the Author

Robert Rohm is a world-class communicator who entertains as he explains key components to relationships and personal development. Dr. Rohm has profoundly impacted the lives of millions of people around the world through his presentations and through his books and tapes.

For nearly 30 years, people have listened, laughed and learned with Dr. Rohm as he pours himself into his high-energy, high-information presentations. He guides people into the principles that they need to improve their communication skills and leadership skills. He also inspires people to greater personal growth and development through his words and his resources.

Dr. Rohm has earned 5 degrees including his Ph.D. at the University of North Texas in Higher Education Administration and Counseling. Dr. Rohm has authored or coauthored several books including *Positive Personality Profiles, Who Do You Think You Are Anyway?, You've Got Style, Different Children Different Needs, Tales Out of School, Get Real!, All about Bots! All about You!, A+ Ideas for Every Student's Success, A Tip in the Right Direction Volume I* and *Volume II,* and *Praying for your Child According to his or her Personality Style.*

Resource Materials

A Tip in the Right Direction
Volumes I, II and III

Life is too short to make all the mistakes yourself! Learn real wisdom from the mistakes of others! Dr. Rohm shares a lifetime of experiences in these easy - to - read books.

These books holds valuable insights that will change your life, and it only takes a couple of minutes a week to gain this powerful knowledge. Join Dr. Rohm as he discusses such topics as: Sometimes you win; sometimes you learn!, A goal without a plan is just a daydream!

You've Got Style

This book is a great introductory book on DISC personality styles. It gives all the basic information about the four personality styles, and it also includes chapters on adapting your style and building better teams.

Positive Personality Profiles

This book gives a basic overview of behavioral styles. It discusses identifying different traits and behavioral preferences for each style. This book provides a foundation for understanding the DISC approach to human behavior. It is written to edify people and give clear understanding on gifts, talents and effectiveness.

Topics covered include: The "Four Temperament" Model of Human Behavior, The "D" type personality, The "I" type personality, The "S" type personality, The "C" type personality, Characterizing qualities, reading people, why opposites attract, classroom scenarios, motivation techniques, practical applications and more .

Praying for your Child
According to his or her Personality Style

All parents want the best for their child. This book walks parents step-by-step into a creative approach to parenting that works with their child's natural style instead of against it. It blends the understanding of personality styles with Biblical principles to produce stronger relationships with happier parents and children.

As you read this book, you will learn how to motivate your child, how to discipline your child and how to truly delight in your child!

The Model of Human Behavior DVD • *PBS Special*

In this fun-filled, fast-paced presentation filmed before a live PBS studio audience Dr. Robert A. Rohm presents the four patterns of Human Behavior. You will never see other people the same way again! Dr. Rohm has a knack for taking complicated issues and breaking them down into understandable concepts that will change your life for the better...forever! Get ready to laugh and learn!

L.E.A.D.E.R.S.H.I.P. By The Letter Audio CD

Get ready to laugh and learn with Dr. Rohm as he explains 10 principles to be an effective leader. Dr. Rohm give secrets on what it takes to be a "true" leader in every situation.

Discovery Report, (Online Assessment)

For adults (Also, available in Spanish and French)

This is a 40 + page report that is personalized just for you. Learn about your own personality style, your ideal environment, your blind spots, your communication style and much more. It begins with an online assessment. After completing the assessment, your Discovery Report is e-mailed to you in about an hour.

Get Real! (Online Assessment for Teens)

This report gives you over 40 pages of specific information for teens. This is one of the most accurate tools available for DISCovering your personality style.

Purpose: This report serves as a guide (like a development handbook) to help teens gain insight into their own motivations, goals and outlook on life.

Description: A personality style analysis for teens designed to define specific personal self-awareness and understanding. Assessment can be compleated in about 15 minutes. The report also lists attributes and occupations associated with personality types.

All About Bots! All About You!
(Online Assessment for Children ages 4-12)

This report gives you over 50 pages of specific information for children ages 4-12. This is one of the most accurate tools available for DISCovering a child's personality style. The information you receive helps a child and his or her parents learn about personality styles.

Purpose: To help parents, teachers and individuals who work with children to better understand them, and for the children to understand themselves and others by explaining personality behaviors and tendencies.

Description: Children look at pictures and read stories selecting the choices that appeal most to them. Stories reveal different styles of behavior. The information generated from the report teaches children how to relate to others as well as understanding the needs of other people. The vital information in this report provides parents and teachers with specific insights to help the child as he or she develops and matures.

We at Personality Insights want to invite you to come to our web site and view the many valuable resources that we make available. We specialize in resources that are particularly related to families, businesses, churches and schools. We also offer many other spiritual, leadership and educational materials. Also, there is a 3 - day training course held in Atlanta, Georgia that you can attend and become a certified Human Behavior Consultant.

Our resources can be ordered by calling

1-800-509-DISC

or visiting

www.personalityinsights.com.

Personality
INSIGHTS
PRESS